D1537712

Myeloma

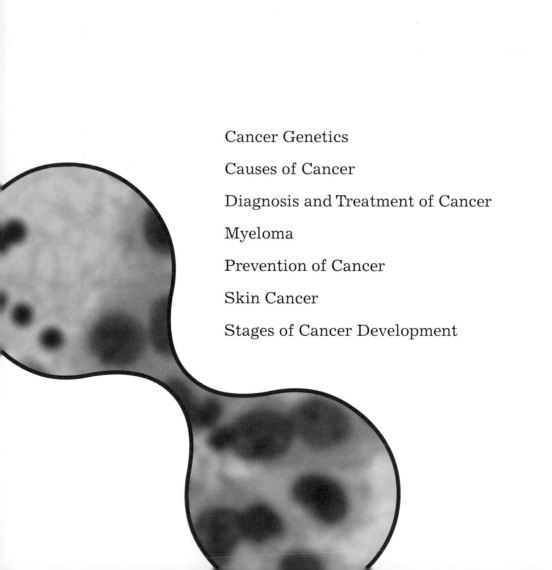

Myeloma

Jerome E. Tanner, Ph.D.

Consulting Editor,
Donna M. Bozzone, Ph.D.
Professor of Biology
Saint Michael's College

CHELSEA HOUSE
PUBLISHERS
An imprint of Infobase Publishing

This book is dedicated to Caroline, my wife, without whose keen eye, help, and encouragement this book could not have been written.

THE BIOLOGY OF CANCER: MYELOMA

Chelsea House
An imprint of Infobase Publishing
132 West 31st Street
New York NY 10001

Library of Congress Cataloging-in-Publication Data
Tanner, Jerome Edward, 1957-
  Myeloma / Jerome E. Tanner ; consulting editor Donna M. Bozzone.
     p. cm. – (Biology of cancer)
  Includes bibliographical references and index.
  ISBN-13: 978-0-7910-8824-1 (alk. paper)
  ISBN-10: 0-7910-8824-3 (alk. paper)
  1. Multiple myeloma. I. Bozzone, Donna M. II. Title.
  RC280.B6T36 2008
  616.99'418–dc22   2007035859

Chelsea House books are available at special discounts when purchased in bulk quantities for businesses, associations, institutions, or sales promotions. Please call our Special Sales Department in New York at (212) 967-8800 or (800) 322-8755.

You can find Chelsea House on the World Wide Web at http://www.chelseahouse.com

Text design by James Scotto-Lavino
Cover design by Ben Peterson
Illustrations by Chris and Elisa Scherer

Printed in the United States of America

Bang EJB 10 9 8 7 6 5 4 3 2 1

This book is printed on acid-free paper.

All links and Web addresses were checked and verified to be correct at the time of publication. Because of the dynamic nature of the Web, some addresses and links may have changed since publication and may no longer be valid.

Herceptin® is a registered trademark of Genentech, Inc. Velcade® is a registered trademark of Millennium Pharmaceuticals.

CONTENTS

◆

FOREWORD

◆

Approximately 1,500 people die each day of cancer in the United States. Worldwide, more than 8 million new cases are diagnosed each year. In affluent, developed nations such as the United States, around one out of three people will develop cancer in his or her lifetime. As deaths from infection and malnutrition become less prevalent in developing areas of the world, people live longer and cancer incidence increases to become a leading cause of mortality. Clearly, few people are left untouched by this disease due either to their own illness or that of loved ones. This situation leaves us with many questions: What causes cancer? Can we prevent it? Is there a cure?

Cancer did not originate in the modern world. Evidence of humans afflicted with cancer dates from ancient times. Examinations of bones from skeletons that are more than 3,000 years old reveal structures that appear to be tumors. Records from ancient Egypt, written more than 4,000 years ago, describe breast cancers. Possible cases of bone tumors have been observed in Egyptian mummies that are more than 5,000 years old. It is even possible that our species' ancestors developed cancer. In 1932, Louis Leakey discovered a jawbone, from either *Australopithecus* or *Homo erectus*, that possessed what appeared to be a tumor. Cancer specialists examined the jawbone and suggested that the tumor was due to Burkitt's lymphoma, a type of cancer that affects the immune system.

It is likely that cancer has been a concern for the human lineage for at least a million years.

Human beings have been searching for ways to treat and cure cancer since ancient times, but cancer is becoming an even greater problem today. Because life expectancy increased dramatically in the twentieth century due to public health successes such as improvements in our ability to prevent and fight infectious disease, more people live long enough to develop cancer. Children and young adults can develop cancer, but the chance of developing the disease increases as a person ages. Now that so many people live longer, cancer incidence has increased dramatically in the population. As a consequence, the prevalence of cancer came to the forefront as a public health concern by the middle of the twentieth century. In 1971 President Richard Nixon signed the National Cancer Act and thus declared "war" on cancer. The National Cancer Act brought cancer research to the forefront and provided funding and a mandate to spur research to the National Cancer Institute. During the years since that action, research laboratories have made significant progress toward understanding cancer. Surprisingly, the most dramatic insights came from learning how normal cells function, and by comparing that to what goes wrong in cancer cells.

Many people think of cancer as a single disease, but it actually comprises more than 100 different disorders in normal cell and tissue function. Nevertheless, all cancers have one feature in common: All are diseases of uncontrolled cell division. Under normal circumstances, the body regulates the production of new cells very precisely. In cancer cells, particular defects in deoxyribonucleic acid, or DNA, lead to breakdowns in the cell communication and growth control that are normal in healthy cells. Having escaped these controls, cancer cells can become invasive and spread to other parts of the body. As a consequence, normal tissue and organ functions may be seriously disrupted. Ultimately, cancer can be fatal.

Even though cancer is a serious disease, modern research has provided many reasons to feel hopeful about the future of cancer treatment and prevention. First, scientists have learned a great deal about the specific genes involved in cancer. This information paves the way for improved early detection, such as identifying individuals with a genetic predisposition to cancer and monitoring their health to ensure the earliest possible detection. Second, knowledge of both the specific genes involved in cancer and the proteins made by cancer cells has made it possible to develop very specific and effective treatments for certain cancers. For example, childhood leukemia, once almost certainly fatal, now can be treated successfully in the great majority of cases. Similarly, improved understanding of cancer cell proteins led to the development of new anticancer drugs such as Herceptin, which is used to treat certain types of breast tumors. Third, many cancers are preventable. In fact, it is likely that more than 50 percent of cancers would never occur if people avoided smoking, overexposure to sun, a high-fat diet, and a sedentary lifestyle. People have tremendous power to reduce their chances of developing cancer by making good health and lifestyle decisions. Even if treatments become perfect, prevention is still preferable to avoid the anxiety of a diagnosis and the potential pain of treatment.

The books in *The Biology of Cancer* series reveal information about the causes of the disease; the DNA changes that result in tumor formation; ways to prevent, detect, and treat cancer; and detailed accounts of specific types of cancers that occur in particular tissues or organs. Books in this series describe what happens to cells as they lose growth control and how specific cancers affect the body. *The Biology of Cancer* series also provides insights into the studies undertaken, the research experiments done, and the scientists involved in the development of the present state of knowledge of this disease. In this way, readers get to see beyond "the facts" and understand more about the process of biomedical research. Finally, the books in *The Biology of Cancer* series provide information to help readers make healthy choices that can reduce the risk of cancer.

Cancer research is at a very exciting crossroads, affording scientists the challenge of scientific problem solving as well as the opportunity to engage in work that is likely to directly benefit people's health and well-being. I hope that the books in this series will help readers learn about cancer. Even more, I hope that these books will capture your interest and awaken your curiosity about cancer so that you ask questions for which scientists presently have no answers. Perhaps some of your questions will inspire you to follow your own path of discovery. If so, I look forward to your joining the community of scientists; after all, there is still a lot of work to be done.

Donna M. Bozzone, Ph.D.
Professor of Biology
Saint Michael's College
Colchester, Vermont

1

AN INTRODUCTION TO MYELOMA

KEY POINTS

♦ Myeloma is a form of cancer that develops from a white blood cell called a plasma cell.

♦ Myeloma cancer cells spread throughout the body to multiple locations in our bones, triggering bone loss, bone pain, and fractures.

♦ Myeloma can cause anemia and fatigue, weaken the immune system's ability to fight infections, and alter normal kidney function.

♦ Although myeloma remains incurable, current medical treatment can alleviate many disease symptoms and extend the lives of patients.

My father, who just turned 67 and is now retired, enjoys golf and seeing his grandchildren growing up. When we were young, Dad worked long hours as a painter to make sure we had the tuition money to get through

11

college. We all knew he really loved his grandchildren, so we made it a point for him to come over every Sunday for dinner.

Recently Dad complained about being tired and having some back pain. We all joked and said, "Dad, why don't you spend a little of your retirement money on a new bed and mattress so you can sleep better?"

My sister, who is a nurse at the university hospital, looked more concerned and spoke to him after dinner. "Dad, perhaps you should go to the doctor and get yourself checked," she said.

Laughing, he remarked, "Hey, it's just a little soreness in these old joints, but if it will make you happy, sure, I'll go; besides it's probably nothing and I can go after I check out the prices on a new mattress."

My dad had his blood drawn for testing by a nurse while the doctor checked his heart and blood pressure, took notes on my dad's weight and asked how he felt generally. Results came back from the medical lab a week later, followed up by another appointment with his doctor. The doctor said he had multiple myeloma, a cancer of the blood. We didn't quite understand what it meant. We all heard the word cancer and recalled what other friends and relatives had to go through when they were treated for their cancers. We wondered what could have been the cause. We also wondered what kinds of treatments were available and if multiple myeloma could be cured.

This fictional case study is typical of someone diagnosed with **myeloma**. Multiple myeloma is a form of **cancer** that originates from **cells** found in the blood called **plasma cells**. Doctors sometimes call this disease multiple myeloma because myeloma cells spread throughout the body to multiple locations in our bones.

A plasma cell is the mature form of **white blood cell** called a **B cell**, which comes from the **bone marrow**, a soft and red fatty tissue that fills the hollow spaces of our skeleton and is the source of our blood cells. Plasma cells are part of a normal **immune system**, helping to protect us from infections. Plasma cells usually make up less than 5 percent of the

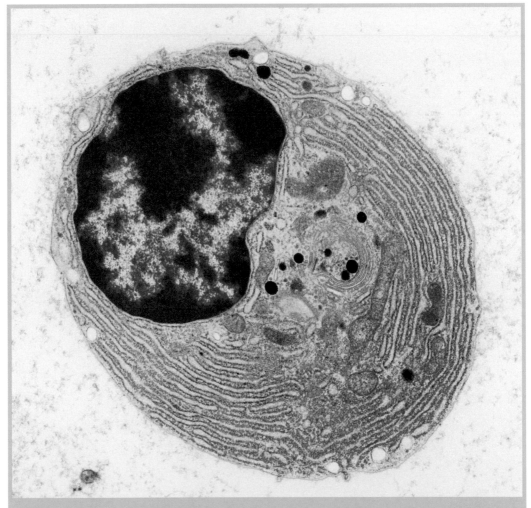

Figure 1.1   Plasma cells are mature B-lymphocytes that produce the immune system's antibodies. These are the cells affected by multiple myeloma. (© *Steve Gschmeissner/Photo Researchers, Inc.*)

cells in bone marrow but, when they change into **malignant** myeloma cells, their numbers can grow to more than 10 percent. At its final or most advanced stage in growth, multiple myeloma spreads uncontrollably throughout the body and lodges in every bone, triggering bone loss, pain, and fractures.

Multiple myeloma also hampers the normal functions of our bone marrow by interfering or crowding out vital blood-forming tissues that produce our red and white blood cells. The loss of healthy bone marrow leads to a low number of red blood cells, a condition called **anemia**, which causes weakness and fatigue, weakens our white blood cells, and increases susceptibility to viral and bacterial infections. Multiple myeloma also triggers a change in kidney function by causing an imbalance in the blood's normal chemistry. Despite recent advancements in cancer therapy and new insights into the biology of multiple myeloma, no currently available medical treatment can offer a true cure. Myeloma patients can however return to near-normal activity with **palliative care**, using drugs to alleviate myeloma symptoms and complications, or undergo **chemotherapy** and bone marrow replacement to extend their lives.

2

INCIDENCE AND RISK FACTORS
FOR MYELOMA

KEY POINTS

- Myeloma accounts for about 10 percent of all blood-related cancers.

- In any given year doctors diagnose approximately 15,000 new cases of myeloma in the United States.

- Myeloma occurrence is highest in people 70 years of age or older.

- With the exception of the syndrome called monoclonal gammopathy of undetermined significance, the exact cause of myeloma remains unknown.

- Obesity, race, and exposure to radiation and petrochemicals increase one's risk of myeloma slightly.

Scientists called **epidemiologists** study the cause and incidence of diseases. Epidemiologists working in hospitals, medical schools, and research laboratories across the country are trying to uncover the cause of

---

◆ CHERNOBYL NUCLEAR ACCIDENT AND THYROID CANCER INCIDENCE IN BELARUS

On April 26, 1986, in what is now the former Soviet republic of Belarus, an explosion occurred at the Chernobyl nuclear power plant that released highly radioactive gas and dust into the atmosphere. This explosion is still regarded as the worst nuclear accident to have ever occurred at a nuclear power plant. The explosion and cleanup of the plant caused 47 deaths and the evacuation and resettlement of more than 300,000 people from the surrounding areas. The explosion caused a radioactive gas cloud that later rained radioactive material all over western Russia, Europe, and North America. It was estimated that as many as 9,000 people among the 7 million people living in the surrounding states of the Ukraine, Belarus, and the Russian Federation were exposed to highly radioactive material from contaminated air and food, which increased their risk of thyroid cancer. Children in the area were particularly susceptible to thyroid cancer because children's thyroid glands are small; in addition, the children's thyroid glands concentrated the radioactive iodine present in contaminated milk. Epidemiologists from Columbia University in New York City screened 13,000 children from the affected areas for the incidence of cancer. They wanted to know whether radioactive iodine caused an increase of thyroid cancer in children. What they saw was a sharp increase in the number of thyroid

multiple myeloma and to think of ways to prevent it. Epidemiologists follow two basic assumptions when they look at the causes of any disease. First, they assume that diseases don't occur randomly but result from a

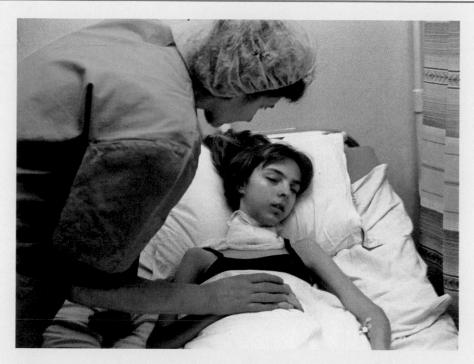

Figure 2.1   This 17-year-old Ukranian girl has just undergone surgery for thyroid cancer. Her exposure as a toddler to radioactive material from Chernobyl was the likely cause of her cancer. *(© AP Images)*

cancers in people of all ages who lived in Belarus, and especially in children. The epidemiologists hypothesized from their data that those children with thyroid cancer likely lacked iodine in their diet, which caused them to be uniquely susceptible to concentrating radioactive iodine in their thyroid and developing cancer.

particular cause. Second, they reason that disease may be prevented if the cause of the disease can be identified.

Epidemiologists studying multiple myeloma are trying to uncover a cause or causes for the disease by asking questions such as:

- Does myeloma occur often in one or more places in the country?

- Do workers in particular jobs get myeloma more often than other workers?

- Is myeloma more common among men or women?

- Do factors like income, race, or ethnicity increase one's chance of getting multiple myeloma?

Epidemiologists answer these and similar questions by comparing two or more unrelated groups of people for a given period of time or, when that is not possible, by observing one group of people over a very long period of time. For practical reasons, rather than gather information from an entire population, epidemiologists instead study subsets of types of people (called samples, or sample sets) who are thought to reflect the characteristics of the entire population. Data are collected from studying these sample sets and subjected to statistical analysis and numerically condensed into averages and percentages or summarized using various kinds of charts and graphs. The statistics compiled from the data allow inferences to be made about the population in general. After reviewing the frequency and disease distribution in the population, epidemiologists then attempt to identify or rule out possible causes of the disease with a goal of telling the public how they might improve their health and lessen the chance of getting myeloma disease.

Looking at population data from the United States, epidemiologists have noticed that myeloma accounts for about 10 percent of all cases of cancers that occur in the blood, and is second in occurrence only to another potentially fatal blood cancer called **non-Hodgkin's lymphoma**. In fact, in any given year, doctors will diagnose nearly 15,000 new cases of myeloma in the United States, and 70 percent of those patients will likely die from the disease without medical treatment.

Beyond simply counting the number of myeloma cases that occur in the United States each year, epidemiologists also want to uncover an exact cause or link to some lifestyle event for the origins of myeloma with the hope that this knowledge might prevent the disease. Let's look at how an epidemiologist approaches this problem by looking at influenza. Influenza, or the flu, has an exact cause and a means of prevention. Medical scientists know that only the influenza **virus**, and no other virus or bacterium, causes the flu. They also know that the flu virus spreads most easily during the winter, a time when people are inside and together. Therefore, scientists reason that to stop the spread of this disease only a vaccine against the influenza virus would work. They can also predict that a flu vaccine would work best to prevent influenza if the vaccine is given before the winter season begins. And so today flu inoculations are given usually between September and November.

Contrast the flu and its direct link to the influenza virus with myeloma. Epidemiologists have yet to find a cause or risk factor that is directly linked to myeloma. Epidemiologists do, however, have some likely suspects that might increase one's risk of developing the disease. Some tantalizing findings from studying various population groups suggest certain risk factors or trends in the U.S. population may be connected to myeloma. Looking at age, gender, race, or lifestyle, it's clear that people near the age of 70 have the highest prevalence of myeloma. Epidemiologists expect that as the large population of baby boomers approach 70 in the coming years, the number of myeloma cases will greatly increase.

Myeloma now accounts for almost 1 percent of all cancers occurring in Caucasians and Asians living in North America, but African Americans are almost two times more likely to develop myeloma than are Caucasians or Asians. In general, men are 50 percent more likely to develop myeloma than women. The risk of getting myeloma also appears to increase with increased body weight. People who are overweight or obese seem to have a higher occurrence of myeloma. To learn whether or not the link between body weight and myeloma will ultimately hold true will require more epidemiological surveys.

The most important predictor for myeloma is a diagnosis of the syndrome called monoclonal gammopathy of undetermined significance (MGUS). Many doctors think MGUS is an early, or "smoldering," form of multiple myeloma. When a person has MGUS, myeloma cancer cells are present in the body but there are so few that a person is unaware of the disease. MGUS is characterized by a high level of antibody in the blood but a normal number of plasma cells in the blood and bone marrow. MGUS occurs in about 3 percent of persons age 70 or older. Myeloma is so closely linked to MGUS that one-quarter of all individuals in the United States diagnosed with MGUS will later progress to multiple myeloma. Fortunately, even for a person diagnosed with MGUS, there may not be a need for immediate medical treatment. Individuals with MGUS can remain symptom-free for years. Doctors do, however, need to monitor them for any myeloma symptoms to decide when to start medical treatment.

Other possible but less likely risk factors for multiple myeloma include a history of myeloma disease in the family, constant exposure to petroleum and petrochemicals, and exposure to high levels of radiation. Based upon a small number of family cases available for study, a prior history of myeloma in a person's family predicts a small but increased risk of developing multiple myeloma in one's children or siblings. People exposed to high amounts of radiation also have an increased risk. Japanese survivors of the atomic bomb blasts at the end of World War II are 10 times more likely to have myeloma or leukemia compared to Japanese of similar age. Because of this finding, scientists have looked at whether smaller amounts of X-ray or nuclear radiation—like those experienced by radiologists and nuclear power plant workers—increase risk of myeloma, but at this time there is no clear evidence linking this level of exposure to an increase in myeloma. Most scientists believe that the risk of getting cancer after exposure to small amounts of radiation such as that received during a dental exam or from medical X rays is extremely small and far outweighed by the medical benefits.

Individuals who make wood furniture and petroleum workers, who are constantly exposed to oil products such as gasoline, paint, or chemicals, have a statistically significant risk of developing myeloma, but the actual occurrence of myeloma in people working in these two occupations is extremely small. Epidemiologists find that people working with petrochemicals or wood have a 0.038 and 0.016 percent increased risk, respectively, of developing myeloma, compared to someone not working in either of these two industries. Other environmental factors or lifestyle factors, such as a person's income, level of education, diet, alcohol consumption, or smoking habit, appear to lack any strong evidence linking them to myeloma.

Despite these findings, there still remain many unsolved mysteries about myeloma and its possible causes for epidemiologists to investigate. Even now epidemiologists are seeing a trend where the number of myeloma cases in people younger than age 55 is increasing. Whether this is because of a new environmental factor or a recent change in people's lifestyle is yet unknown, but it is hoped epidemiologists will soon find answers to the question of risk factors and the causes of myeloma.

Figure 2.2 Exposure to radiation from atomic explosions at the end of World War II increased tenfold the incidence of myeloma and leukemia in survivors of the blasts. (© *Science Source/Photo Researchers, Inc.*)

SUMMARY

Epidemiologists, who study the incidence of disease in the population, find that myeloma occurs most in people who are near 70 years of age and a higher number of cases occur in men than women. The disease appears twice as often in African Americans than in Caucasians or Asians and may be linked to obesity. Chances of getting myeloma may also be linked to family history and exposure to high levels of radiation or petrochemicals, but the increased risk is extremely small. In fact, with the exception of MGUS, people who develop myeloma have no common risk factor or underlying cause linking them with their illness. For now the cause of myeloma remains a mystery, but with the information gathered by epidemiologists and physicians, a possible cause or risk factors may be found to prevent this disease.

3

BIOLOGY OF MYELOMA

KEY POINTS

♦ Myeloma is a white blood cell cancer that is derived from cells called plasma cells.

♦ Plasma cells are mature B cells; B cells are part of the immune system, which makes antibodies to fight infection.

♦ Myeloma cells have an abnormal amount of DNA, have changes to their DNA, and have lost the ability to stop growing.

♦ Myeloma is characterized by an overproduction of antibody protein and bone loss.

♦ Myeloma causes bone loss and bone marrow destruction, leading to bone fractures and a weakened immune system.

Myeloma is a plasma cell **neoplasm**, which is a new and abnormally growing tissue. Many neoplasms are **benign** and show little or no harmful effects. Warts are an example of a benign neoplasm. Warts are caused by the papilloma virus. Skin cells infected with the papilloma virus grow abnormally but only form a harmless mound of bumpy skin. Warts do not invade deep into the skin or spread to other organs. Myeloma, on the other hand, is a malignant neoplasm that grows and spreads to many distant sites and organs. Any cell or tissue in the body can become a malignant neoplasm, including blood cells and plasma cells.

Plasma cells are the final growth stop in the life cycle of a normal white blood cell called a **B cell** or **B-lymphocyte**. B-lymphocytes produce **antibodies**; they are one of the most sophisticated weapons in an immune system's arsenal.

THE DIFFERENT TYPES OF ANTIBODIES

Antibody molecules can bind to a host of different things, ranging from small viruses and cancer cells to much larger objects like ragweed pollen and dust particles. Each antibody molecule is shaped like the letter Y and made up of two identical, large proteins and two identical, small proteins. The two large proteins are called the antibody heavy chains and the two smaller proteins are called the antibody **light chains**. The names *heavy* and *light chains* come from experiments done in the 1960s. At that time, scientists wanted to identify the various components of blood. They found that if they put protein from plasma into a tube of sugar water and spun that tube at very high speeds, the centrifugal force made the proteins separate into two layers in the tube. One layer of protein was found at the bottom of the tube and so it was called the heavy protein. The other protein layer was located at the top of the tube and was referred to as the light protein. Years later these two protein layers were found to contain the large and small proteins that make a complete antibody molecule.

Antibody proteins are normally bound together by small molecular bridges made of sulfur atoms to form a single Y-shaped molecule, but sometimes the Y-chains are stitched together into two or five antibody molecules.

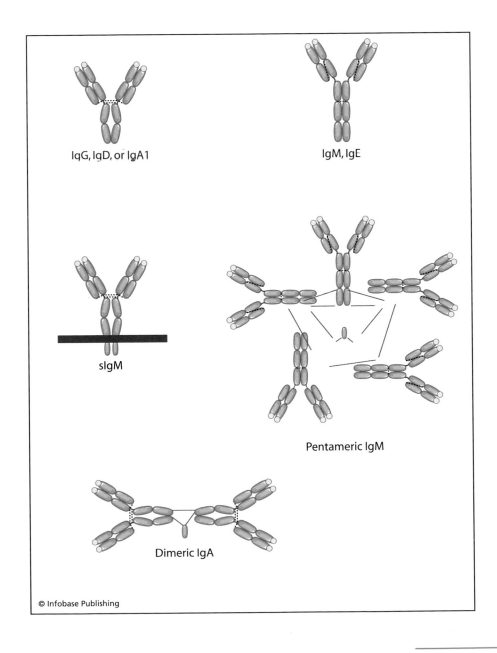

IgG, IgD, or IgA1

IgM, IgE

sIgM

Pentameric IgM

Dimeric IgA

♦ LAB TESTS ON A COMPUTER CHIP?

In the not-so-distant future yearly physical exams may consist of nothing more than mailing a drop of blood to a doctor. Scientists are developing computer chips called **DNA** chips, or DNA microarrays, which can spot subtle changes in **genes**, the basic units of inheritance that tell cells how to make proteins, or detect just one or two cancer cells among the million or more cells contained in a drop of blood. Using their knowledge of the entire human genome sequence and the thousands of genes linked to cancer, scientists have copied and placed minute amounts of these cancer genes, called DNA probes, onto glass slides no bigger than a piece of gum. The DNA chips work through a chemical process called DNA hybridization. A cancer DNA probe will fluoresce, or light up, whenever a strand of cell DNA containing the same cancer gene recognizes and binds to the DNA probe. Scientists can now check for any genetic changes against the thousands of known cancer genes in just a few hours, a process that would have taken weeks or months before the invention of DNA chip technology. The advantage of DNA chips is that doctors can now look at a large number of genes for any sign of cancer and make a better choice from the selection of drugs used to treat cancer.

These less common antibodies, called IgM and IgA, have the ability to bind to many similar molecules at once or to selectively concentrate in the lungs or nasal cavities. Although all antibody molecules share many

Figure 3.1 *(opposite page)* In the human immune system, Y-shaped antibody molecules attach to foreign substances, such as viruses or cancer cells. Unlike other antibodies, IgM and IgA antibodies can bind to many similar molecules at once.

common properties, the heavy and light chains that make up each and every antibody molecule are not identical. Every antibody molecule has two small sets of uniquely individual protein sequences, located at the tips of their Y-shaped molecule, that distinguishes one antibody from one another. These unique sequences are called the antibody variable regions. They give each antibody molecule the ability to recognize and bind to one and only one particular molecular sequence or shape called an **antigen**, or **epitope**.

LIFE CYCLE OF A B CELL

Given the diversity of germs and molecules found in nature, antigens can come in millions of different shapes and chemical combinations, but to fit into the antibody binding site, they can be no bigger than the size of five sugar molecules linked end to end. So when an antibody sticks to a bacterium, it is attached to a very, very small piece of a bacterium's surface, indeed.

B-lymphocytes come from bone marrow found in the ribs, leg bones, and bones in the spine. In many ways, bone marrow is like a major industrial center, crowded with many different blood **cell** factories, each with cells having special functions and working capabilities. Some of these cells, called **reticular cells**, provide structural support and form the building frames for bone marrow tissue while others, called **stromal cells**, provide young, developing red and **white blood cells** with timely nutrients and signals that allow them to grow and mature properly.

Figure 3.2   *(opposite page)* An antibody molecule, showing its sulfur bridges and how it binds to antigens.

The earliest or first cell from which B cells or all other white and red blood cells begin is called the hematopoietic (blood) **stem cell**. Stem cells are **pluripotent**, meaning that they have the ability to develop into

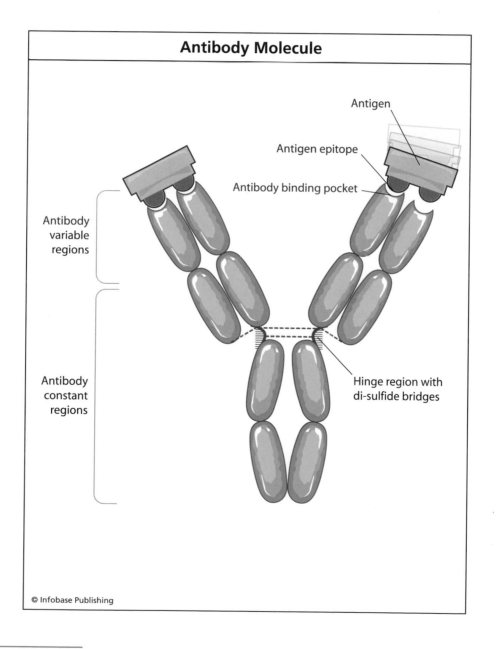

Antibody Molecule

Antigen

Antigen epitope

Antibody binding pocket

Antibody variable regions

Antibody constant regions

Hinge region with di-sulfide bridges

many different types of cells. A blood stem cell can just as easily develop into a red blood cell or one of the many different kinds of white blood cells. The earliest kind of B cell that comes from a blood stem cell is called a **pro-B cell** or **pre-B cell**; it is usually found next to the inner surface of the bone marrow cavity called the **subendosteum**. A young B cell is committed to become a B cell but is still immature and can only make antibody heavy chain protein. As it matures and once it produces light chain proteins and assembles them into complete antibody molecules, it can be called an immature B cell. Although immature B cells are found in high numbers in the bone marrow, their life span is surprisingly short. It is estimated that most immature B cells live for only two to four days and that only a small fraction will ever survive to become a mature B cell. Scientists estimate that from an initial 20 to 40 million pre-B cells, only 5 to 10 percent will live to become mature B cells. At first glance, this type of B cell production looks very inefficient. Why would the immune system go through all the trouble of making young B cells, only to throw them away? One reason might be that they incorrectly rearranged their antibody genes and produced defective antibody. If a B cell does not express antibody properly, it signals itself to die. A second reason might be that the young B cell reacted to the body's own tissues. This is also a strong signal for the B cell to die.

It would be impossible for a single B cell to make the billions of different kinds of antibody needed to match and protect against the millions of different germs and harmful agents found in the environment. Therefore, B cells have a unique system in which antibody genes, small pieces of DNA that provide B cells with instructions on how to produce

Figure 3.3 *(opposite page)* The life span of a B cell is short, and most immature B cells do not become mature B cells.

the antibody molecule, are correctly shuffled and glued together to code for a unique, one-of-a-kind antibody molecule. Scientists estimate that shuffling and gluing all the different combinations of possible antibody

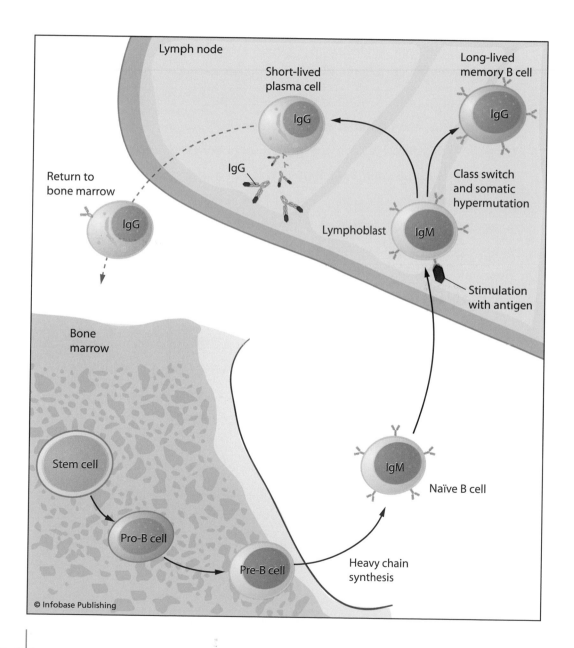

© Infobase Publishing

genes could generate at least 10 trillion (1 with 13 zeros after it) unique, one-of-a-kind antibody molecules.

These genes that code for the different pieces of antibody are far apart. In fact, they are found on entirely different **chromosomes**. A human B cell has 23 duplicate or diploid pairs of chromosomes, numbered 1 to 22, along with a pair of sex chromosomes called X and Y, for a total of 46 chromosomes. Each chromosome contains enough genetic information to code for hundreds of different proteins. The genes for the antibody light chain protein are located on a chromosome numbered 22 while the genes that code for the antibody heavy chain protein are located on a chromosome numbered 14.

Scientists think the final set of antibody genes that will code for heavy and light chain proteins are formed once DNA, spanning thousands of DNA sequences, forms big loop-like structures that are cut and then glued properly back together by B cell enzymes, called the **VDJ recombinase complex**.

If a B cell has fully matured and no longer needs help from bone marrow stromal cells, it leaves the bone marrow and takes up residence in the spleen or lymph node and waits with its customized antibody to bind to any matching antigen that passes by. **Lymph nodes** and their larger cousin, the spleen, a large, dark-red, oval organ located on the left side of the body between the stomach and the diaphragm, are filled with white blood cells. One might imagine white blood cells of the immune system swimming hurriedly throughout the circulatory system in a chaotic and unmanageable way, but this is not the way it works. Mature white blood cells are housed mainly in the lymph nodes and spleen and use the circulatory system only as a major thoroughfare to go from lymph node to lymph node or spleen and back to lymph node. Blood is filtered through the spleen or lymph nodes that are located

◆ CHROMOSOMES: THE MASTER PACKERS OF THE CELL

DNA molecules do not exist in cells, as often depicted in illustrations, as a naked, double-stranded helical string. Instead, cellular DNA is encased with many different nuclear proteins to form a substance called chromatin. To get an idea of how much DNA can be packed into a cell's 46 chromosomes, imagine this: If one takes the DNA from just one human cell, strips it of all its nuclear proteins, stretches it out, and lays it end to end, it would extend to more than six and a half feet. Amazingly, all this DNA is stuffed into the cell's nucleus, a space 11 times thinner than the width of a human hair. Packing DNA into chromatin is accomplished by proteins called histones and numbered as H1, H2A, H2B, H3, and H4. Together these five histones form ball-shaped protein structures called nucleosomes, which contain many positively charged residues, or **amino acids**, that allow negatively charged DNA to easily wrap around them. Chromatin viewed with a powerful electron microscope seems to look like a long string of beads. When the cell is ready to divide and its entire DNA has doubled, the cell tightly coils and coils its chromatin into higher-order structures seen in the microscope as chromosomes. Chromosomes then line up in the middle of the cell before being equally divided into two new and identical cells called daughter cells. These new daughter cells uncoil their chromosomes into chromatin and go on to perform their daily functions making protein, synthesizing DNA, and waiting for a time in the future when they are ready to divide again.

at strategic points throughout the body, such as in the mouth (tonsils), the nasal sinuses, the lungs, and near openings of our urinary and digestive systems. When our bodies are combating a severe infection, the white blood cells in lymph nodes are very active and can cause the lymph nodes to swell and feel tender. If you ever went to a doctor complaining of a sore throat and general fatigue, the doctor may have felt the lymph nodes in your neck to see if they were enlarged or painful. This can give an indication of how well your immune system is fighting the infection.

If a mature B cell living in the lymph node binds to its proper antigen, it will grow and divide many times to make thousands of identical B cell clones called a **plasmablasts** (also called lymophoblasts). Plasmablasts sometimes undergo one final genetic fine tuning of their antibody genes, which involves a focused alteration or trimming of the antibody variable region gene segments called **somatic hypermutation** before they finally transform into a plasma cell. Somatic hypermutation changes the antibody gene code in such a way that the antibody now binds more strongly to its antigen.

Plasma cells are like "miniature antibody factories," whose sole function is to make large amounts of antibody. It is estimated that one plasma cell can make two thousand antibody molecules per second. Because an antigen-activated B cell, such as one stimulated by a virus or **bacteria**, divides into thousands, if not millions, of identical B cell clones, it is easy to understand why a high level of antibody is found in blood within just a few days after any viral or bacterial infection. Myeloma is a malignant plasma cell neoplasm and so behaves like any plasma cell. The trouble is that it does not know when to stop dividing and so it produces excessive amounts of unwanted antibody that builds up in the blood.

Figure 3.4   *(opposite page)* Lymph nodes house B cells and other white blood cells and are the major centers of the body's immune system.

THE LIFE CYCLE OF A MYELOMA CELL

Although the earliest events that cause a plasma cell to transform into a myeloma cell are unclear, scientists do know that the myeloma cell

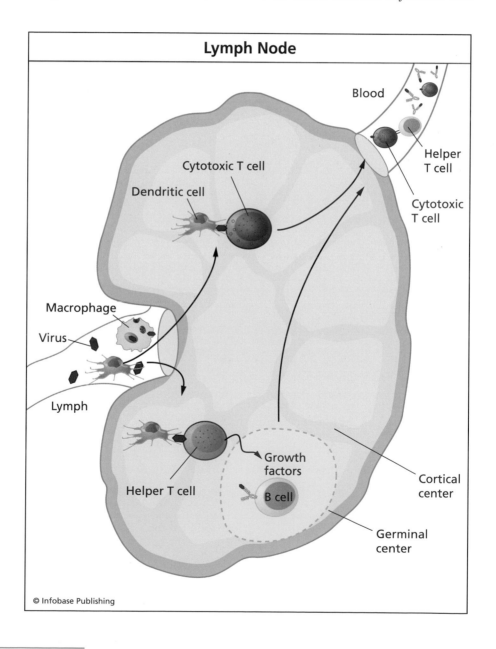

♦ THE LYMPH NODES AND CANCER

Keeping your shoes on can help fight infections. Did you know that your feet are the only part of the body that has no lymph nodes? Lymph nodes and the spleen make up what is called the lymphatic system, a vital part of the immune system that helps the body fight infections or screen for cancer. The lymphatic system consists of a network of thin-walled venous structures connected to bean-shaped lymph nodes. Lymph nodes become swollen or inflamed whenever resident white blood cells are actively fighting bacterial infections or cancer. Physicians usually biopsy (surgically remove for microscopic examination) enlarged lymph nodes from a cancer patient that have been swollen for more than a month or two as they may harbor cancer cells. Examination of an enlarged lymph node can tell the doctor how advanced the cancer is or whether a particular cancer treatment has been effective at reversing cancer cell growth.

---

originates from a single B cell that once resided in a lymph node or spleen. When doctors specializing in blood disorders, called hematologists, remove a bone marrow sample called a bone aspirate, or biopsy, containing myeloma cells and look at them under a microscope, they often see a high number of plasma-like cells that contain both an abnormal number and gross changes in their chromosomes. About 7 out of 10 people diagnosed with myeloma have chromosomal changes in their cancer cells. They also notice that myeloma cells often have an unusually high number of mutations in their antibody genes, which appear to have occurred during the somatic hypermutation event.

Most myeloma cells also have an extra chromosome, called **chromosome trisomy**, instead of the normal two copies. Often chromosomes in a myeloma cell are also mixed-up, with a piece of

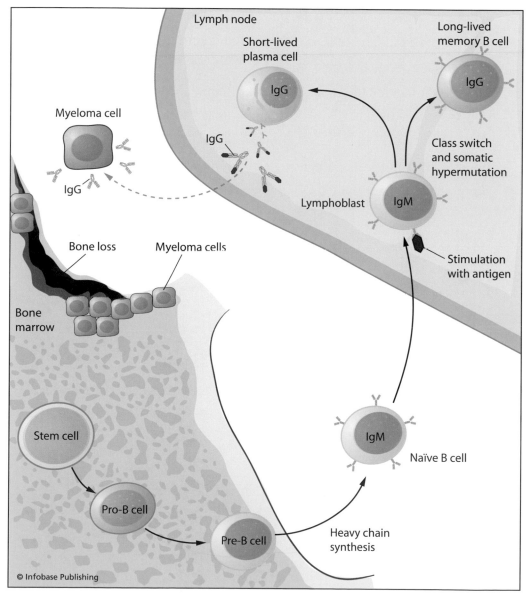

Figure 3.5   Myeloma originates with a mutation in the plasma cell.

one chromosome stuck onto an entirely different chromosome. These chromosome mix-ups always involve the antibody heavy chain gene, located on chromosome 14, and a piece of chromosome 4, 6, 11, 16, or 20. The attachment of the antibody heavy chain gene to another chromosome appears to be the first critical event in the transition of a normal plasma cell into a myeloma cell, because these chromosome changes are even detected in MGUS, the earliest stage of myeloma disease. Some scientists speculate that these chromosomal mix-ups cause uncontrolled cell growth, meaning that the normal mechanisms that signal the plasma cell to stop dividing have failed. While it isn't known what all these changes mean just yet, they are helpful in predicting how patients will respond to medical treatment.

Plasma cells are normally found in small numbers in the bone marrow, but because myeloma cells won't stop growing, they overcrowd and damage healthy bone tissue. At this stage myeloma lesions are found in only one or a few sites in the bone by X-ray examination. Doctors call this stage of myeloma the intramedullary (inside the bone) stage. As the disease progresses and myeloma cells spill out of the bone marrow and into the circulation, they lodge themselves in other bones' cavities throughout the body. Doctors called this the **extramedullary** (outside the bone) stage. At the extramedullary stage, the cancer is so advanced that there is little likelihood of recovery. The various steps in myeloma development are summarized in Figure 3.6.

Not all the symptoms and complications caused by myeloma can be attributed to too many myeloma cells. An individual myeloma

Figure 3.6   *(opposite page)* The progressive stages of myeloma.

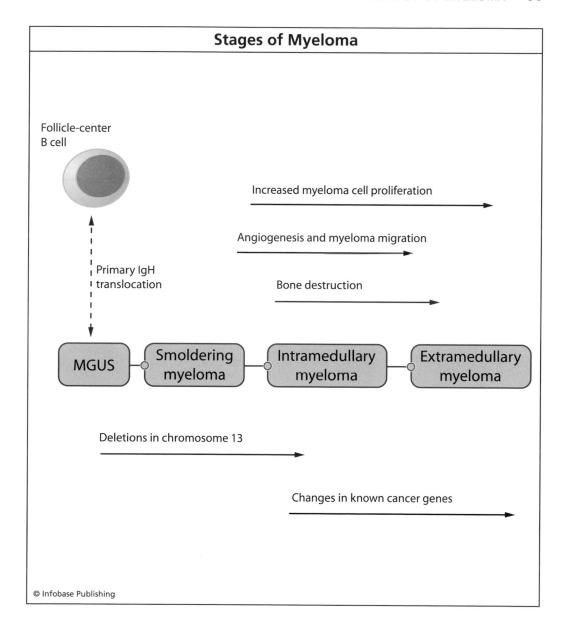

Stages of Myeloma

Follicle-center
B cell

Primary IgH
translocation

Increased myeloma cell proliferation

Angiogenesis and myeloma migration

Bone destruction

MGUS — Smoldering myeloma — Intramedullary myeloma — Extramedullary myeloma

Deletions in chromosome 13

Changes in known cancer genes

cell also influences adjoining bone and bone marrow cells, leading to bone loss or fractures, as well as to abnormal increases in blood calcium from lost bone tissue. Healthy bones are constantly repairing themselves. After weeks of exercise, just like muscles, bones become thicker and stronger. This is because bone cells called **osteoclasts** are removing old and weakened bone tissue while bone cells called **osteoblasts** are filling these weak spots with additional calcium and minerals.

The cycle of bone removal and bone addition by osteoclasts and osteoblasts is normally in perfect balance. However, myeloma cells cause osteoclasts to be more active and tip the normal balance in favor of them and bone loss. At the same time that myeloma cells are causing bone loss, they also stimulate bone marrow stromal cells to produce growth factors called **lymphokines**, which promote myeloma cell growth. Three of the most important myeloma-growth lymphokines are **vascular endothelial growth factor (VEGF)**, tumor necrosis factor-alpha (TNF-α), and **interleukin-6 (IL-6)**. VEGF encourages the growth of new blood vessels that supply hungry myeloma cells with oxygen and nutrients. Interleukin-6 and TNF-α work together to make myeloma cells grow faster and spread to other bones. When TNF-α is overproduced, it can cause white blood cells to die. It can also lower the production of red blood cells by blocking a red blood cell **hormone** called **erythropoietin**. The loss of red and white blood cells from TNF-α causes anemia and reduces the immune system's normal ability to fight-off viral and bacterial infections. In fact, after bone loss, bacterial infections are the second most common problem caused by myeloma.

Figure 3.7   *(opposite page)* Myeloma interferes with the cycle of bone removal and addition. This causes bone loss and lesions.

SUMMARY

Myeloma is a progressive cancer derived from a type of B cell called a plasma cell. Myeloma is characterized by excessive numbers of plasma

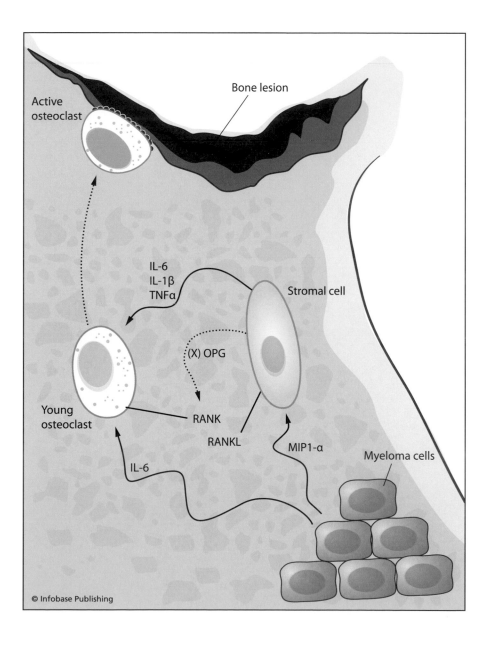

© Infobase Publishing

cells in the bone marrow and the overproduction of antibody. Myeloma stimulates bone marrow cells to produce growth factors called lymphokines that promote the creation of new blood vessels and promote cancer growth and cancer spread. Eventually the increased numbers of myeloma cells cause the destruction of healthy bone and bone marrow tissue. Bone loss and damage to bone marrow increases susceptibility to infection.

4

THE IMMUNE SYSTEM AND CANCER

KEY POINTS

- Blood is composed of red blood cells, plasma, and white blood cells of the immune system.

- The immune system is an intricate collection of specialized white blood cells, tissues, and organs that protect us from infections and eliminate cancer cells before they can grow into malignant tumors.

- Leukocytes called macrophages and natural killer cells form the innate arm of the immune system and are the first cells to recognize and kill cancer cells.

- Lymphocytes called B and T cells form the adaptive arm of the immune system and eliminate cancer cells using customized detectors that recognize small pieces of protein called epitopes on the surface of a cancer cell.

Although epidemiologists have discovered that MGUS is an important predictor of myeloma and medical scientists are beginning to understand where myeloma comes from and why it acts as it does, scientists still must find answers to important questions, such as "How does our body protect us from this disease?" To find the answer we will explore how blood components and the immune system work together to fight cancer.

Our bodies are under attack every day from a variety of toxins, germs, or even cancer cells. We breathe air that is saturated with smoke, dust particles, spores, pollens, and chemical fumes. We eat leftovers found in the refrigerator that might be teeming with bacteria, or unknowingly touch a cold or flu virus left behind on a door handle by a sick student, or even have our own cells turn against us and become cancer. Every day we encounter a barrage of germs or produce defective cells whose sole function is to stay alive and frustrate the body's defenses. How is it that we win battle after battle against disease or fend off cancer when the opposing teams seem to have all the advantages of time and numbers? The answer lies in our body's remarkable defense mechanism called the immune system. Most of us take for granted this intricate collection of specialized cells, **tissues**, and **organs** whose sole purpose is to detect, tag, and destroy foreign invaders. Although myeloma cells were once healthy, normal cells, they are viewed by the immune system as invaders and destroyed in healthy individuals before they have a chance to settle in and grow into malignant **tumors**. Cancer or infectious germs come in many varieties, forms, and types. How exactly does our immune system know what belongs and what does not? Are we born with a complete set of blueprints housed in immune cells for disease recognition or

◆ ANY BLOOD WILL *NOT* DO

The idea that blood contains "the living force" of the body to overcome disease was a belief held even in ancient Roman times. Romans thought that blood possessed mysterious curative properties and that it held a person's mental and physical qualities. The Roman scholar Pliny the Elder wrote, "If someone drank blood out of a loving cup he would be cured of epilepsy or if he drank the blood of a dying gladiator he would gain his strength and bravery." Today such notions are considered absurd, but misconceptions about blood such as these persisted even into the late nineteenth century. As late as the 1880s, doctors injected cow or goat milk into a sick person's veins in an attempt to restore their blood's vitality. This practice was quickly abandoned when people became sick or died from these infusions.

In the early 1900s, Dr. Karl Landsteiner discovered that mixing red blood cells from one person with the serum from another person sometimes caused the red blood cells to clump. Through these types of experiments, Dr. Landsteiner was able to sort everyone's blood into three groups that he called A, B and C (C was later renamed O). This discovery dispelled the notion that "any blood will do," and allowed blood transfusions between people sharing the same blood type to become widespread, the safe common practice we still use today. Every year nearly 5 million people in the United States receive life-saving blood transfusions to replace blood lost after severe accidents or to alleviate anemia caused by cancer or chemotherapy.

◆ RED BLOOD CELLS: FACTS AND FIGURES

Ateaspoon of blood contains about 4 to 5 million red blood cells. Compare this with white blood cells, which number only 4,000 to 11,000 cells per teaspoon of blood. If you lined up end-to-end the 20 to 30 trillion red blood cells contained in your body they would circle all the way around the Earth's equator. A red blood cell contains about 270 million iron-containing **hemo-globin** molecules. When oxygen from the lungs binds to the iron atom in hemoglobin, it causes the red blood cell to change to the bright scarlet color seen in arteries from the more bluish color found in oxygen-devoid red blood cells circulating in our veins. Red blood cells last for about four months. To keep up the body's demand for red blood cells, bone marrow must continually produce red blood cells—at a rate of about 2 million cells per second.

---

does the immune system draft a plan every time we encounter a new and threatening cell or **microbe**?

BLOOD COMPONENTS

If you have ever cut yourself and taken a good look at your blood, it may have appeared to be just a thick, red, homogeneous liquid. But if you placed some of that blood in a tube and spun the tube at a very high speed in a centrifuge machine, you would see that the blood is no longer a solid red color but forms three distinct layers in the tube.

Figure 4.1   *(opposite page)* The components of blood are red blood cells, white blood cells, and plasma.

At the bottom of the tube, and taking up almost half of the tube's space, are the red blood cells, also called **erythrocytes**. Occupying the top half of the tube is an opaque, yellow liquid called **plasma**.

Blood Components

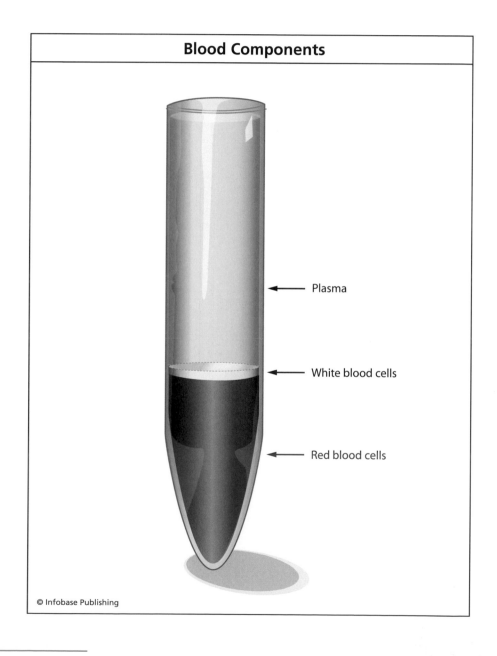

Plasma

White blood cells

Red blood cells

Plasma contains **platelets**, which make blood clot, along with minerals, nutrients from digested food, and two important immune system weapons called **complement** and antibodies (also called immunoglobulin or gamma globulin).

Complement is a set of blood proteins originally made in the liver that can make holes in bacteria or cancer cells by allowing liquid to rush in from the outside, causing the bacteria or cell to pop like exploding balloons. Healthy body cells are protected from complement by **molecules** on their surface that deactivate complement. Besides punching holes in cells and bacteria, complement also attracts white blood cells, called macrophages, to the sites of infection or cancer. Once complement sticks to the surface of a bacterium, any nearby macrophage will go on the offensive to envelop the bacterium by **phagocytosis**. Later the bacterium is slowly digested in acids and digestive enzymes present in the macrophage's **cytoplasm**.

The last component of blood visible in the test tube is a thin, white, fluffy layer of cells. This layer is sandwiched between the erythrocytes and the plasma layer. Scientists call this thin layer the **buffy coat**. The buffy coat is where all the different types of white blood cells that make up the immune systems can be found. Seen through a microscope the live white blood cells taken from the buffy coat appear small, clear, and uncomplicated. But white blood cells are anything but simple in nature. Depending on their origins, white blood cells come in two types, a **leukocyte** and a **lymphocyte**. After studying individual leukocytes and lymphocytes, scientists have found that the leukocytes and lymphocytes work much like a tag-team wrestling pair,

Figure 4.2   *(opposite page)* The immune system has two arms, the innate and the adaptive.

with leukocytes forming half of the immune system, called the **innate immune system**, and lymphocytes comprising the other half, called the **adaptive immune system**.

Cells of the Innate Immune System		Cells of the Adaptive Immune System	
Cell type	**Function**	**Cell type**	**Function**
Macrophage	Phagocyte and scavenger	Helper T cell	Aids cytotoxic T cells Aids B cells to make antibodies IL-2
Dendritic cell	Antigen presentation	Cytotoxic T cell	Killer of virus-infected cells
Neutrophil	Phagocyte	B cell	Synthesizer of antibodies
NK cell	Killer of virus-infected cells and cancer cells		

THE INNATE IMMUNE SYSTEM

Leukocytes of the innate immune system form the first barrier against any germs that manage to get past our protective skin. If you have ever injured your skin and experienced the pain, redness, and swelling of an infected cut, you have experienced leukocytes and the innate system hard at work. Leukocytes also act as sentinels to detect and alert the immune system to the presence of cancer cells. Leukocytes come in three different cell types called macrophages, **neutrophils**, and **natural killer (NK) cells**. These three cell types can be distinguished from lymphocytes by their lumpy-looking nucleus or a grainy-looking cytoplasm. Both macrophage and neutrophils are "hardwired" with a pre-set detection apparatus called Fc receptors on their cell surface, which are especially sensitive in detecting cells or bacteria coated with antibodies or complement. Macrophages generally lie resting on the inner linings of blood vessels, crevices throughout the body or linger in our spleen, lungs, and liver, whereas neutrophils circulate in the blood. Neutrophils are normally found in low numbers in the blood, but during a severe bacterial infection, the bone marrow quickly ramps up neutrophil production to increase their numbers. When a doctor says, "Your white blood cell count is up," what he or she is really telling you is that your neutrophil cell count is up in the blood, likely because of a bad bacterial infection. Once excited by a bacterium or cancer cell, these two cells signal a call to arms in the form of protein messengers called lymphokines. Lymphokines are made by many white blood cells and comprise a family of 30 or more unique and small hormone-like proteins that act like homing beacons and cell growth stimulants to draw other white blood cells to the site of infection or cancer. They cause white blood cells to multiply rapidly to stop a microbe or cancer cell from gaining a further foothold in the body. Sometimes after macrophages have eaten a virus, bacterium, or fragments of a dead cancer cell, it transforms into a new form of cell called a **dendritic cell**. Dendritic cells help bridge the innate and adaptive arms of the immune system by displaying pieces of digested microbe or the abnormal proteins made in cancer cells on their cell surface to tell lymphocytes of the adaptive arm exactly what type of virus, bacterium, or cancer is present.

The third principal cell in the innate immune system is a natural killer (NK) cell. NK cells, as their name implies, will kill any cell that shows evidence of cancer or disease. NK cells, like macrophages and neutrophils are hardwired, too, but with different detectors, allowing NK

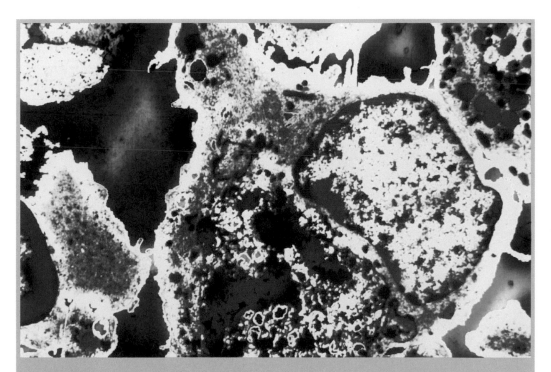

Figure 4.3 Macrophage cells defend the body against infection by consuming foreign microorganisms through a process called phagocytosis. *(© Meullemiestre/ Photo Researchers, Inc.)*

cells to distinguish a normal cell from an abnormal one. They act like nervous security guards who constantly bother fellow body cells, asking their one question: "What's the password?" If the cell correctly presents the right password, known as **human leukocyte antigen (HLA)**, the NK cell relaxes and says "Okay, move along." Any defective cell that does not give the proper password will unleash the NK cell killer response. NK cells kill by triggering a self-destruct mechanism called **apoptosis**, or programmed cell death in an abnormal cell. Since NK cells can distinguish a cancer cell from a healthy one, medical scientists are now trying to boost both the number and the effectiveness of NK cells in cancer patients by giving injections of two NK-promoting lymphokines called **interleukin (IL-2)** and **interferon-α**.

THE ADAPTIVE IMMUNE SYSTEM

As good as the innate immune system may be at stopping infections or cancer, it cannot shield us completely. This is where the adaptive immune system comes in. The T- and B-lymphocytes make up the adaptive immune system. Unlike cells of the innate immune system with their static, hardwired recognition systems, T and B cells have the ability to form customized detectors. We have already looked at the B cell detectors, namely, the antibody molecule, and how they are made. T cell detectors are called **T cell receptors**. T cell receptors are found on the surface of T cells and made from two proteins called the alpha chain and the beta chain. Although the T cell receptor is completely different from the antibody molecule, the T cell receptor is constructed in a similar fashion from a pool of receptor genes that are shuffled and glued together like the antibody molecule. T cell receptors, like antibodies, recognize and bind to similar small epitopes. A

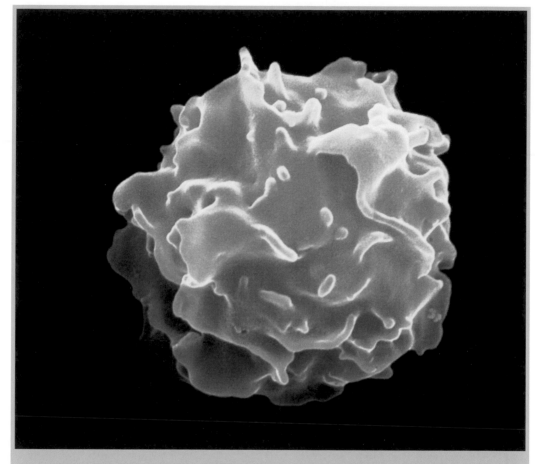

Figure 4.4 Natural killer (NK) cells will detect and kill abnormal or foreign cells, because those cells do not possess the human leukocyte antigen (HLA), which is unique to each person's body. (*© Eye of Science/Photo Researchers, Inc.*)

cancer cell epitope may be malformed protein or one that contains errors in its sequence, which came about from genetic mutations. Once a T- or B-lymphocyte recognizes a cancer cell epitope, it divides into thousands of identical clones, making its own specialized receptor or antibody, respectively.

◆ DEATH BECOMES YOU!

Apoptosis is now recognized as an important biological process that occurs in plants and animals. Apoptosis occurs as the leaves change color and fall off trees in the autumn, when a tadpole loses its tail and grows into a frog, and in the formation of fingers and toes in a developing fetus. Apoptosis is also used to eliminate worn out cells or cancerous cells with DNA damage. Every year, humans lose their body weight in cells through the process of apoptosis such that at any mo ment millions of cells are dying and removed from the body. Apoptosis also plays a role in cancer; if a cell is unable to undergo apoptosis, due to mutation or biochemical inhibition, it can continue dividing and develop into a tumor. Scientists are now developing new types of drugs called antisense DNA that can block the synthesis of a key protein, called Bcl-2, found in the apoptosis machinery. It is hoped that blocking the synthesis of Bcl-2 protein will re-instill apoptosis and cause the cancer cell to die.

T cells, unlike B cells, come in two types, one is called a **helper T cell** and the other is called a **cytotoxic T cell**. Although they appear similar under the microscope, one can tell the difference between a helper T cell and a cytotoxic T cell by the protein "ID card" that each T cell displays on their cell surface. Helper T cells carry the ID protein called CD4; its job is to help B cells make more antibodies by providing B cells with growth-promoting lymphokines. Cytotoxic T cells, on the other hand, carry the CD8 protein ID card. Cytotoxic T cells are the "enforcers" of the adaptive immune system. Like NK cells, their job is to eliminate any defective cancer cells or ones infected with a virus. Cytotoxic T cells, like NK cells, stop cancer cells by activating that same self-destructing, apoptosis button in the cancer cell.

All T cells are born in the bone marrow but go to the thymus gland to grow and mature. The **thymus** is a butterfly-shaped gland that is found at the base of the neck just above the heart. Helper T cells and cytotoxic T cells are trained very early in their development to detect and react to T cell epitopes found on microbes or cancer cells. The thymus gland is where all T cells undergo their education before becoming functional T cells. T cells learn only one lesson in the thymus, namely, to answer the question, "Who are you and what are we?" Scientists call this the immune system's ability to tell "self from non-self." It is very important that all T cells learn this lesson, otherwise they wouldn't know the difference between foreign protein and virus molecule (a "non-self" molecule) from "self" molecules like ones made from the body's own cells and tissues. Any T cells that fail to distinguish a self protein from and non-self protein are destroyed. This is to avoid the disaster of confusing a normal cell with one infected with a virus and thus kill or damage healthy tissue. In some rare genetic diseases certain faulty T cells manage to escape the thymus and destroy the body's healthy tissue. Juvenile or type I diabetes is a disease where epitopes on insulin producing cells in the pancreas are mistaken for a virus because these faulty T cells could not tell the difference between self and non-self.

It might seem that matching the right B or T cell with its counterpart antigen or epitope and the following expansion of these B and T cells into thousands of identical clones would take a long time. Well, it does! In fact it takes several days for a person's immune system to make a sufficient number of T cell and B cells that can recognize and fight back against an infection. This is why our immune system relies so heavily on its innate defense arm as the first-response team. Recall that the macrophage and NK cells, along with complement, do not require prior exposure to recognize bacteria or cancer cell. Complement can immediately punch holes in cancer cells while NK cells can join in the fight and kill as many cancer cells and give the adaptive immune system enough time to make T cells and antibodies, and keep the cancer from taking hold.

SUMMARY

The immune system, which is comprised of the innate arm and adaptive arm, is constantly vigilant to defend us against common infections and prevent cancerous cells from taking hold. NK cells and macrophages from the innate arm are the first line of defense against cancer by constantly checking cells for their changes in expression of HLA, which is a sign it may be cancerous. Cytolytic T cells and antibodies made by B cells form the adaptive arm of the immune system. It protects us from cancer by detecting cancer epitopes, using customized receptors called the T cell receptor and the antibody molecule.

5

CLINICAL FEATURES AND DIAGNOSIS OF MYELOMA

KEY POINTS

♦ Doctors initially use blood tests that measure calcium, the cell waste product creatinine, myeloma antibody, called M protein, and antibody fragments called Bence Jones protein to check for and monitor myeloma.

♦ X-ray or MRI images and CAT scans are used to locate bone lesions caused by myeloma or myeloma tumors in soft tissues.

♦ Based on blood tests and medical imaging, myeloma progression, or staging, is grouped using two systems: the Durie-Salmon Staging System or the International Staging System.

♦ Accurate cancer staging is crucial to determining appropriate treatment.

Individuals at an early stage of myeloma often have no major symptoms of the disease. They may experience a general feeling of fatigue or have vague complaints. Often their myeloma is only discovered following a routine medical exam and a laboratory check of their blood and urine. Most ill patients come to the doctor complaining of pain in the lower back or ribs, or a severe sudden pain from a fracture or compression of a bone in their spine. People with later stage myeloma commonly have anemia and persistent fatigue, loss of weight and appetite, bone pain and bone loss, weakness or numbness in their legs, bacterial infections, a low number of white blood cells, or a need to drink or urinate often because of changes in their blood or kidneys. These symptoms will vary in occurrence and extent among different people and are often confused with other diseases or health problems. If a person over age 50 experiences any of these symptoms, he or she should consult a doctor.

If a doctor hears a description of such symptoms and suspects multiple myeloma, the physician will begin by measuring the amount of antibodies in the patient's blood. The test for antibody as well as the testing of other important blood components requires the removal of a small amount of blood (generally 10 to 20 milliliters or 0.5 ounce) from the arm. This blood sample can be taken during a routine physical exam. The doctors will also test for the presence of, or changes in, other blood proteins, blood salts and minerals, plasma cell numbers, or possible genetic or chromosomal changes in bone marrow plasma cells.

Almost 80 percent of people with myeloma have high concentrations of a single kind of antibody in their blood. Doctors call this single antibody myeloma protein, or **M protein**. Recall that even after a plasma cell has transformed into a myeloma, it still thinks and acts like a plasma cell and so continues its job of making large amounts of antibody. Sometimes the plasma cell cancer makes more light chain protein than can be assembled into an antibody and dumps this excess light chain protein into the blood and urine. Doctors call this excess light chain protein the **Bence Jones protein** after its discoverer, English physician Henry Bence Jones who described it in 1847. About 3 out of 4 people with malignant myeloma have high amounts of Bence Jones protein in their blood and urine. Excessive M protein can have dire consequences. M protein can thicken the blood, which reduces blood flow to the brain and causes headaches and blurred vision, or it can cause increased bruising and nose bleeds. Bence Jones protein causes blood clots in the arms, legs, kidneys, eyes, and heart, which ultimately lead to kidney problems, loss of vision, heart disease, and numbness in the arms and legs because of nerve damage.

If the doctor sees a large amount M protein, he or she would see the first solid indication that the patient has either myeloma or its early form, MGUS. To measure M protein in the blood, medical laboratories separate M protein from other blood components using a technique called **electrophoresis**. Electrophoresis is widely used to separate large blood proteins from small ones. Electrophoresis works much like paper chromatography experiments that students sometimes perform in basic science class. It is based on the idea that protein building blocks called amino acids have positive or negative charges when placed in an acid or base solution. Because different types of proteins will have different numbers and kinds of charged amino acids, proteins can be separated from the mixture if first put in an acid or base buffer and then run in an electrical field. Proteins will move toward the appropriate electrode according to their overall electrical charge and size. After electrophoresis, one identifies the different blood proteins by using colored dyes that stick exclusively to proteins. What one sees after electrophoresis of blood plasma from a myeloma patient is a huge colored band where antibody protein is normally found.

The amount of antibody in 3 ounces of blood from a healthy person is about 1 gram (less than the weight of a quarter of a teaspoon of salt). In advanced myeloma disease, M protein increases five times to 5 grams per 3 ounces of blood. If the doctor sees such high amounts of M protein, he or she will ask if the patient feels tired or has experienced recent infections; will check the number of red and white blood cells; and especially check for the number of neutrophils, which combat bacterial infection. Doctors know that high numbers of myeloma cells slow down the production of red blood cells and weaken white blood cells, which increase a patient's chances of acquiring a bacterial infection.

The most common type of M protein antibody made by myeloma cells is called immunoglobulin-gamma or IgG, and the second most common M protein is called immunoglobulin-alpha or IgA. The presence of IgG or IgA is often associated with different myeloma symptoms. Myeloma cells making IgA are more often found in the blood, whereas myeloma cells that make IgG are most often in the bone. Electrophoresis of blood plasma can also be used to measure any changes in M protein over time. This allows doctors to monitor M protein and track the progress of the disease and perhaps assess how well the patient's myeloma is responding to drug treatments. If M protein levels are going down after drug treatment, the drugs are working but if M protein rises after therapy, the cancer is coming back.

Figure 5.1 *(opposite page)* Doctors use electrophoresis to determine the levels of myeloma (M) protein in the patient's body.

The doctor also checks the blood for calcium, the amount of waste products, and certain kinds of blood proteins. Calcium is the most plentiful and one of the most important minerals in the body. The body

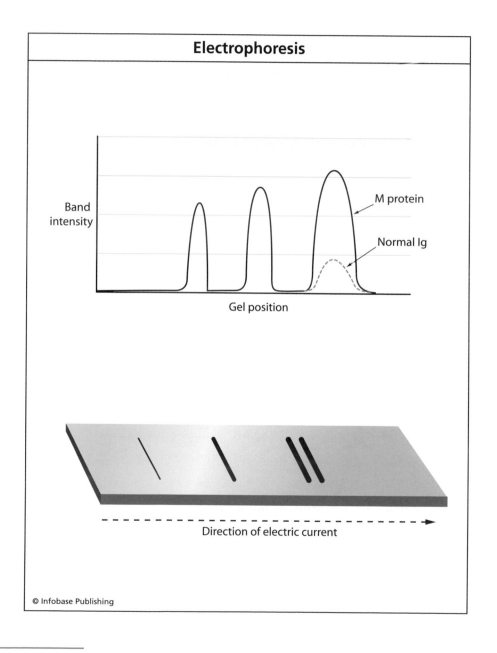

Electrophoresis

Band intensity

M protein

Normal Ig

Gel position

Direction of electric current

needs calcium to repair and build bones and teeth, help nerves work properly, contract muscles, clot blood, and maintain heart rhythm. Almost all the body's calcium is found in bones. Under normal conditions the level of calcium in the blood is carefully controlled by bone cells and only small amounts are released into the blood and urine. The normal concentration of blood calcium ranges from 9 to 10.5 milligrams per 100 milliliters of blood. That's equivalent to a few grains of salt in 3 ounces of liquid. When myeloma causes osteoclasts to remove bone, it causes bone calcium to be released into the blood and results in the syndrome called **hypercalcemia**. Hypercalcemia is found in about 30 percent of people who have myeloma. High calcium interferes with kidney function and causes the patient to feel the constant need to drink and urinate. High calcium can also interfere with the nervous system and cause mental confusion. Doctors rely on tests that measure calcium because it is easy to take blood samples in the office, and the tests are very sensitive and quick to give an indication of bone loss. The doctor also will check the levels of **creatinine** in the blood. Creatinine is a metabolic waste product that is removed from the body by the kidneys. If the levels of creatinine are high in the blood, the kidneys may not be functioning properly.

Recently doctors have been looking at two new blood tests to detect and follow myeloma. One test checks for the level of a protein called β_2**-microglobulin**, normally found on the surface of white blood cells and shed into the blood in low amounts. However, when myeloma cells increase, they cause white blood cells in the bone marrow to die, releasing β_2-microglobulin into the blood. Doctors use the amount of β_2-microglobulin to gauge the numbers of myeloma in the bone marrow. A second blood test recently used by doctors checks for the amount of blood protein called **albumin**. Albumin is normally made by the liver and excreted into the blood. Albumin acts as a blood transporter of hormones and other small molecules; its levels are thought to reflect the overall health of a cancer patient. Low levels of albumin are an indication of worsening patient health.

A less commonly used blood test measures a protein called **C-reactive protein**. Like albumin, C-reactive protein is produced by the liver. The liver makes large quantities of C-reactive protein whenever the myeloma growth factor interleukin-6 is found at high levels in the blood. Because high levels of interleukin-6 causes myeloma cells to grow faster or increase liver production of C-reactive protein, C-reactive protein can act as a surrogate indicator of interleukin-6 and myeloma growth.

TESTING FOR BONE LOSS

If the blood tests positive for M protein or the other blood proteins are positive, the physician will first suggest that the patient go to the hospital to have X-ray pictures taken of their bones.

X-ray machines use a powerful form of energy called electromagnetic energy. Electromagnetic energy is made up of light particles called photons. Photons come in different energies, from the high-energy photons called gamma rays and X rays, to visible light photons that color our world, and finally to low-energy photons in the form of microwaves and radio waves. X-ray photons contain so much energy that an X-ray beam can pass right through most parts of the body. Like shadows produced when one stands between a bright light and an adjacent wall, X rays can outline our dense bone material from our softer, less dense muscles. A typical X-ray image is a shadow image of the X rays that passed through the softer tissues and ones that were blocked by dense bone tissue. If you pass X rays through the body and let them hit a piece of X-ray sensitive film, the film can detect the amount of X-ray energy that passed through the body and reveal a negative silhouette of your bones and tissues.

◆ THE DISCOVERY OF THE X RAY

On November 8, 1895, Professor Wilhelm Conrad Roentgen was working late in his laboratory. He was a professor of physics in Germany working with a new piece of equipment he had obtained from a colleague, called a Lenard cathode ray tube. Although much more powerful, the Lenard cathode ray tube is similar in looks and function to the picture tube found in televisions. Working alone on that Friday evening in a darkened lab, Professor Roentgen was trying to repeat some of the earlier experiments performed with the cathode ray tube by Dr. Lenard. Roentgen was fascinated by the Lenard tube's ability to send a stream of energy, called cathode rays, through the open air. Roentgen had set up his cathode ray tube just like other times, but on this particular night things were a little different because the lab was dark. He had also covered the tube with cardboard to keep out any outside light. Moreover, he happened to leave a piece of glass painted with a fluorescent material just a few feet away on the table. When he turned on the machine he suddenly noticed a shimmering green light coming from the table. He could not believe his eyes, so he repeated the experiment again and again. Each time he turned on the tube he got the same shimmering green light. Excited, he soon realized the green light was coming from the piece of painted glass. Professor Roentgen did not know what was causing the green fluorescent light, so he hypothesized that it was caused by some new and unknown

Doctors can see if bone tissue has gotten thin or where myeloma cells have accumulated from X-ray images. X-ray images of the bones of a myeloma patient show bone damage as darkened patches (dark areas

type of energy, which he called X for "unknown." Roentgen spent the next eight weeks working and sleeping in his laboratory, trying to see if these new X rays could travel through different media besides air. He tried dense objects like wood or light objects like paper and noticed that the fluorescent intensities were different, depending on how dense or thick the object was. One time, when he held a disc of lead between the tube and the glass screen, he absently-mindedly kept his hand there and was astonished see not only the lead disc, but an outline of the bones of his thumb and forefinger. He immediately called his wife, Bertha, to come to the lab to show her this amazing discovery. Together they repeated the experiment, but this time she placed her hand between a photographic plate and he shined the X rays at her hand. Bertha and Wilhelm were excited as they developed the film. They could see the outline of her hand, the bones inside, and even the dark shadow of her wedding ring. Bertha and Wilhelm could see the bones in her hand because X rays have the ability to easily pass through lightweight tissues like skin and muscle, but are blocked by dense tissues such as bones. Bones block X rays, so bones will look transparent on film. Other, less dense tissues, such as lungs and muscle, allow X rays to easily pass through and expose the film. That's why they look gray or black in appearance on a radiograph film. Today X-ray machines are mainly used to check for broken bones but are also used to check for bone thinning or localized bone lesions in cancer patients.

on X-ray film are where the X rays passed through unimpeded). Doctors know that if they detect significant bone loss after an X-ray exam, if the patient has already lost 50 percent of his or her bone mineral, that patient would be late in the course of myeloma disease. Approximately 75 percent of patients who go to the hospital to check for suspected myeloma disease will show some evidence of bone loss on their X rays.

One problem with X-ray procedures is that the patient must be constantly turned because larger bones often block the visibility of smaller underlying bones. Doctors working with engineers overcame this problem by moving the X-ray beam instead of the patient. Moving the X-ray beam is the basic idea behind the **computerized axial tomography (CAT)** scanning machine.

CAT scan machines use normal X-ray imaging technology but move the X-ray beam and X-ray detector in three dimensions. This allows doctors to see the outline of bones and organs in three dimensions. CAT scans are more sensitive than X-ray films because they reveal more details of bone loss in a myeloma patient. The CAT scan machine looks like a giant donut. The patient lies on a table in the center of the donut and the X-ray beam emitter, which is mounted on the donut ring structure, moves around the body of the patient. The X-ray detector that is located directly opposite the X-ray emitter feeds its information directly into a computer. During a CAT scan the X-ray beam moves in a circle all around the patient, taking hundreds of X-ray pictures from different angles to generate a three-dimensional computer image of internal organs and bones. With detailed three-dimensional images of the patient, doctors can more safely perform bone biopsies because they get an idea where

Figure 5.2 *(opposite page)* An X ray takes a picture from a single angle. *Inset:* This X ray shows the damage done by myeloma as darkened patches.

myeloma is located in the bone. This is especially important if the bone biopsy is from the spine, where a mistake in needle placement could permanently damage spinal nerves.

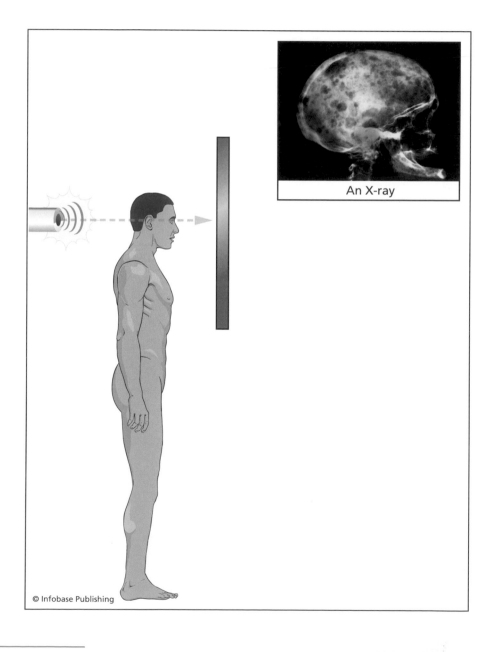

An X-ray

© Infobase Publishing

Sometimes the physician needs to look at a myeloma tumor that is found in soft tissues like the bone marrow that won't show up on X-ray films or CAT scans. In order to overcome this problem doctors use

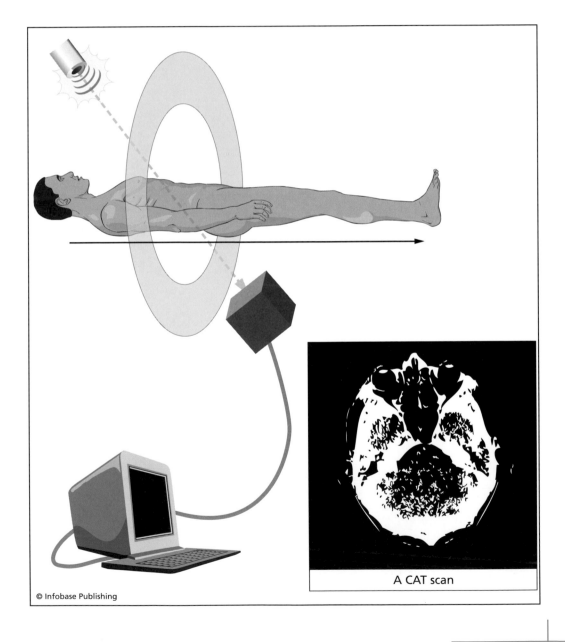

A CAT scan

magnetic resonance imaging (MRI) machines. MRI machines use a completely different type of technology from X rays or CAT scans. Unlike X-ray film or CAT scan machines that detect high-energy electrons, MRIs measure changes in the spin of hydrogen atom **protons**. Protons are the positively charged particles found in the nucleus of all atoms.

Our bodies contain billions upon billions of hydrogen atoms, whether they are attached to proteins or other molecules, or in the form of water. The proton of a hydrogen atom is always spinning, much like a toy top. It spins normally in any direction. However, if the hydrogen atom proton is near a strong magnetic field, such as the MRI machine, the hydrogen atom proton begins to spin in a direction perpendicular to the MRI's magnetic field. MRI machines are so strong they can generate a magnetic field that is 10,000 to 40,000 times more powerful than the Earth's magnetic field. When a patient enters the MRI machine, the hydrogen atom protons in his or her body begin to spin in a direction perpendicular to the MRI's magnetic field. For a person who is lying down in the MRI machine, this means the protons spin in the direction of his or her head or foot (that is, they will spin ← or →). For 99.9999 percent of the hydrogen protons, half will spin in the direction of the head (←) and half will spin in the direction of the feet (→). In doing so, the two spin directions will cancel out each other. Fortunately, for every million or so hydrogen atoms, there will be a hydrogen atom whose proton spin does not match the other 99.9999 percent of hydrogen atoms. This one-in-a-million hydrogen atom may not seem like very much until one counts the roughly 4×10^{27} hydrogen atoms (that's 4 x 1 followed by

Figure 5.3   *(opposite page)* A CAT scan generates a three-dimensional image. *Inset:* This CAT scan shows a large myeloma bone lesion.

27 zeros) found in the body. Therefore, these one-in-a-million hydrogen atoms amount to quite a large number. Once all the hydrogen protons are lined up by the magnet, the MRI machine sends out a short radio

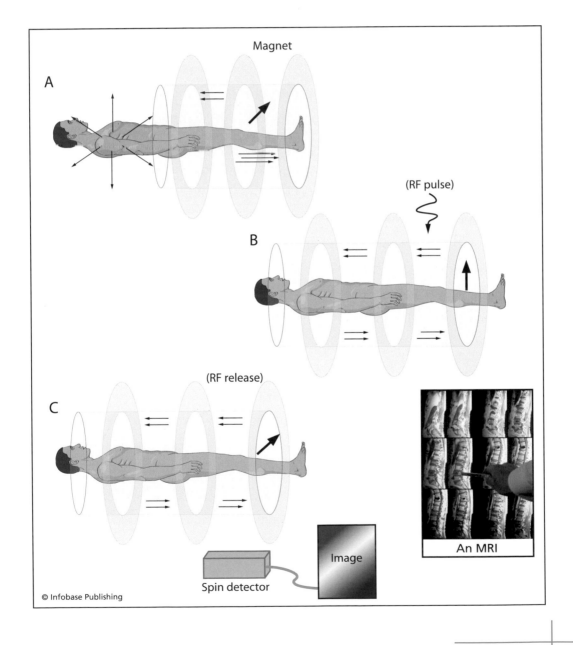

© Infobase Publishing

beam to a millimeter-sized point inside the patient's body. These radio waves are tuned to match the spin frequency of a hydrogen proton. When the hydrogen proton feels the energy, it absorbs the radio waves and is nudged into a different spin direction. The absorption of radio waves by the hydrogen proton is called the "resonance" phase, which constitutes the origin of the name magnetic resonance imaging. Almost immediately, the radio signal is turned off. This causes the hydrogen proton to fall back into its old spin direction, releasing the radio energy it absorbed. The release of radio energy by the one-in-a-million hygdrogen atoms is felt by highly sensitive radio detectors and used to generate a three-dimensional image of the body.

MRI images are far superior to X rays and CAT scans because they can provide a detailed view of all the soft tissues in the body, such as the liver, intestines, and bone marrow. Magnetic resonance images can detect bone loss and bone marrow problems in 86 percent of patients who have myeloma.

MYELOMA CLASSIFICATION AND CLINICAL STAGING

The medical diagnosis and stage of myeloma growth is based on the number of plasma cells in the bone marrow, the presence of M protein in the blood or urine, and the degree of bone loss. Patients are also classified into categories, or stages, according to the number and severity of their clinical symptoms. While there may be some overlap between the various myeloma stages, the classification process is important because

Figure 5.4 *(opposite page)* An MRI provides the most accurate picture of the body. *Inset:* An MRI image shows the soft tissues as well as bone.

it allows the doctor to develop more effective drug treatment plans or to predict a patient's potential outcome following drug treatment.

While some people with myeloma may not need immediate treatment, others may require therapy as soon as possible following the diagnosis. Myeloma patients are classified into three groups: MGUS, smoldering myeloma, and multiple myeloma.

MGUS is an asymptomatic condition whereby the only abnormal sign is the presence of high levels of M protein in the blood or urine. However, unlike the later stages of myeloma, plasma cells in MGUS appear normal in number. MGUS patients show no major symptoms that would explain the increase in M protein. MGUS may ultimately advance to myeloma, but it may take months or years. MGUS is characterized by high M protein, normal numbers of plasma cells in the bone marrow (less than 10 percent), and absence of anemia, hypercalcemia, or bone damage. There is no specific treatment for MGUS. Patients are checked periodically for an increase in M protein or the onset of myeloma-related symptoms such as bone pain or anemia.

Individuals with smoldering myeloma not only have high levels of M protein but also show a slight increase in the number of plasma cells in their bone marrow. They may have mild anemia or a few bone lesions, but they do not have severe bone pain, kidney problems, or frequent bacterial infections. Like MGUS, patients with smoldering myeloma may not advance to multiple myeloma for months or years. At the smoldering myeloma stage the doctor will check for new symptoms, generally every three months. The doctor may prescribe a drug called **bisphosphonate** at this time to slow bone loss, or other drugs to relieve bone pain or treat anemia. In smoldering myeloma, patients having at least one bone lesion may progress to advanced myeloma within one year. Consequently, most doctors start chemotherapy treatment at this time.

TABLE 5.1 MYELOMA STAGING SYSTEMS		
	DURIE-SALMON STAGING SYSTEM FOR MYELOMA	INTERNATIONAL STAGING SYSTEM
Stage I: Early Myeloma	• Hemoglobin level 10 g/dL[a] • Blood calcium level < 10.5 mg/dL[b] • X ray shows no bone destruction • Only one or two plasma cells • Low M protein	• β_2-microglobulin < 3.5 mg/dL and serum albumin > 3.5 g/dL
Stage II: Intermediate Myeloma	• Blood test and X ray results lie between stage I and stage III	• Neither stage I nor stage III
Stage III: Late Myeloma	• Hemoglobin level < 8.5 g/dL • Blood calcium level >12 g/dL • X rays shows two or more big bone lesions • High M protein level • Kidney problems • Blood creatinine (a waste product) is high	• β-2-microglobulin > 5.5 mg/dL
Subclassification (A or B)	A: Normal kidney function B: Abnormal kidney function	
453 grams ~ 1 pound • dL (desi-liter ~ 3.3 ounces) • 1 mg = 1/1000 gram		

Patients with symptomatic multiple myeloma have very high M protein levels along with a sharp increase in bone marrow plasma cells. These symptomatic patients also have signs of anemia, kidney malfunction, increased blood calcium, and several bone lesions. Patients at this stage of the disease need immediate treatment to slow progression of the cancer.

Doctors also divide myeloma disease into stages using either the Durie-Salmon System or the ISS (International Staging System) (Table 5.1). The Durie-Salmon System uses the different symptoms and panel of tests discussed above to classify patients, while ISS uses only the β_2-microglobin and albumin blood tests that were discussed earlier. When measured together, levels of β_2-microglobin and albumin provide a greater ability to predict a patient's overall health in comparison to the Durie-Salmon System. The ISS can also assist the doctor when gauging how aggressive the treatment can be without causing undue harm to the patient. If the two ISS tests tell the doctor that the albumin levels are normal and the patient is relatively healthy, the doctor can more confidently proceed with strong doses of chemotherapy. If, however, β_2-microglobin is high and albumin is low, the doctor knows that the patient has high numbers of myeloma cells and may be too weak to withstand a strong chemotherapy.

SUMMARY

Most people go to the doctor when they first suspect a health problem. The doctor will ask about their symptoms, when they occur, and whether anything makes them better or worse. The doctor will first recommend some simple blood and urine tests that check for abnormal levels of the antibody M protein and antibody fragments called Bence Jones protein if myeloma is suspected. Blood calcium and creatinine levels will also be measured to see whether myeloma is causing bone loss or lessening kidney function. Recently doctors are using a blood test to measure albumin or β_2-microglobulin proteins to aid in predicting how advanced the cancer may be. To see whether myeloma is increasing bone loss or causing bone damage, whole body X-ray pictures are taken, and if one or more bone lesions are found, a CAT or MRI scan is performed. All this information from blood tests and medical imaging helps doctors determine the stage of the disease and allows them to decide on the best treatment program.

6

CURRENT TREATMENT
OPTIONS FOR MYELOMA

KEY POINTS

♦ Myeloma treatment is often limited to palliative care, which minimizes the symptoms of the disease.

♦ Chemotherapy can be used to treat advanced myeloma.

♦ Following chemotherapy, patients undergo an infusion of healthy blood marrow, either from samples of their own marrow taken prior to treatment or a transplant from a genetically compatible donor.

Generally speaking, any person diagnosed with myeloma but not experiencing severe symptoms will likely be monitored for signs of worsening disease on a continuing basis. The doctor will watch for increases of M protein in the blood. Typically the time interval between an initial diagnosis of myeloma disease and the beginnings of severe myeloma symptoms is two to three years. Patients who are first diagnosed with myeloma but show few if any symptoms or complications are given palliative treatment. Palliative treatment means supportive care and drugs will be given to relieve a patient's symptoms but the myeloma itself will not be treated. Doctors may prescribe drugs to relieve bone pain or prescribe drugs called bisphosphonates to help stop bone loss. If the disease appears to be advancing rapidly, the doctor may recommend immediate and more aggressive medical treatment.

PALLIATIVE CARE

Because myeloma can cause a number of complications, doctors need to treat each complication differently. Patients with myeloma often experience pain, anemia, and bacterial infections. The patient is prescribed drugs or a care program to eliminate or stabilize these different problems, while trying to slow down the progression of the myeloma.

Bone Pain

Bone loss due to myeloma can cause severe pain, bone breaks, and bone fractures in the arms, legs, or spine. Doctors may give aspirin or acetaminophen if the pain is not too disabling. Stronger pain-relieving drugs called **opioids** may be prescribed for cases of severe pain. The opioid class of drugs includes **opium** and **morphine**. These are powerful sleep-inducing and pain-relieving compounds prescribed as codeine, oxycodone, or morphine. If bone loss or fractures occurs in the arm or leg bones, chemotherapy or radiation treatment is sometimes used to eliminate myeloma cells that are causing the problem. Sometimes bone fractures are glued together by a procedure called **vertebroplasty**. Vertebroplasty is often used to strengthen bones of the spine and involves the injection of a cement-like mixture, similar to dental filling, through a long needle.

Bone Loss

As discussed in an earlier chapter, myeloma increases osteoclast destruction of bone tissue. Bisphosphonates are drugs used to prevent the bone-chewing activity of osteoclasts and allow the affected bone to regenerate and repair itself. Bisphosphonates are also used to lower blood calcium.

Radiation therapy is an important treatment for bone loss and bone pain. Generally, doctors use radiation on small targeted areas of bone where damage is severe. Radiation therapy uses focused beams of high-energy in the form of gamma rays or X rays on specific areas of bone. The focused X-ray beams break myeloma chromosomes and DNA and prevent the cells from dividing. While radiation therapy can quickly shrink a small myeloma lesion that is causing the severe pain or bone loss, doctors try to avoid treating large areas of bone with radiation because such treatment can permanently damage neighboring bone marrow tissue and prevent that part of the bone from making new blood cells.

Anemia

Anemia is seen in more than 65 percent of patients diagnosed with myeloma. It is caused by myeloma cells crowding out and damaging healthy bone tissue. Anemia can also occur after chemotherapy treatments or from the effects of myeloma on the kidneys. Kidneys not only remove waste products from the blood but also produce erythropoietin. Erythropoietin is a hormone that stimulates bone marrow to make red blood cells. If a myeloma patient has severe anemia, the doctor may give blood transfusions or injections of erythropoietin two to three times a week to increase the number of red blood cells.

Infections

Bacterial infections are the leading cause of death in myeloma patients. Both myeloma and chemotherapy weaken the immune system and cause a patient to become prone to bacterial infections. Doctors normally prescribe antibiotics to help treat or prevent bacterial infections in myeloma patients.

Kidney Problems

As mentioned in an earlier chapter, M protein or Bence Jones protein cause kidney damage in myeloma patients. Signs of kidney damage include dehydration, hypercalcemia, urinary infections, or high levels of

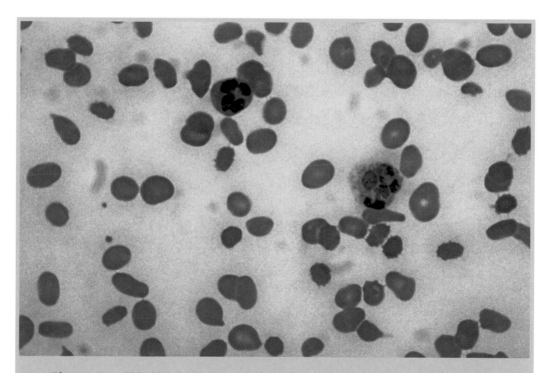

Figure 6.1 This blood smear comes from a person with anemia. Anemic blood has far fewer red blood cells than normal blood. Anemic red blood cells are also often enlarged or deformed. (© Dr. E. Walker/Photo Researchers, Inc.)

metabolic waste products in the blood—a condition known as hyperuri-cemia. Doctors try to boost kidney function and alleviate dehydration by giving fluids or mineral supplements to lower blood calcium. If kidney damage is severe, the doctor may recommend **hemodialysis**. Hemody-alysis is a medical procedure that uses a dialysis machine to cleanse the blood of waste products.

TREATMENTS FOR MYELOMA

No current medical treatment offers a cure for myeloma, but many myeloma patients can return to near-normal activity after being treated. In recent years chemotherapy and bone marrow transplantation have been used to improve the health of myeloma patients, free them of bone pain, and allow them to live longer lives. Chemotherapy is given in three steps, or stages. The first of these is called the induction step. The second is the plateau step. The third step is known as the refractory, or relapse, stage. Relapse occurs when the cancer no longer responds to medical therapy and has returned. In people who are younger than 65 and just diagnosed with myeloma, doctors start chemotherapy treat-ment at the induction step. This step attempts to lower the total number of myeloma cells in the body with the hope that the disease will stabilize and not advance further. If the disease does remain stable, the patient is said to have attained the plateau step. Doctors use strong doses of chemotherapy to get from the induction step to the plateau stage. Che-motherapy treatment is considered a success if the patient becomes free

Figure 6.2 *(opposite page)* Hemodialysis cleanses the blood using a dialysis machine. This is done when the kidneys are too damaged to perform this essential function. *(Andrei Malov/ iStockphoto, Inc.)*

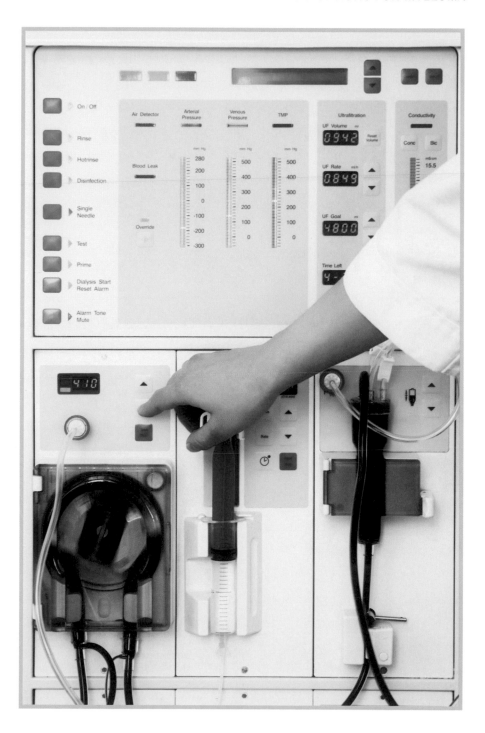

of symptoms, such as fatigue or bone pain, or if M protein blood levels remain either stable or are lower for at least six months after treatment. Chemotherapy starts with three to four injections of a chemotherapeutic drug over a period of 12 to 18 months. The chemotherapeutic drug used most often is called **melphalan**. This drug blocks cells from dividing and decreases the number of myeloma cells in the body. During this time some of the patient's healthy bone marrow is removed and frozen for use after chemotherapy. Melphalan is harmful to both myeloma cells and bone marrow cells because it cannot distinguish between a dividing myeloma cell and a dividing bone marrow cell. Like many other

♦ FROM DEADLY MUSTARD GAS TO MEDICAL MIRACLE

Modern cancer chemotherapy can be traced directly back to World War I and chemical warfare agents, such as mustard gas. Mustard gas, along with chlorine and phosgene gases, destroys the lungs and causes serious blistering of the skin or internal organs. These chemical agents killed more than 90,000 soldiers and maimed more than 1.2 million soldiers in World War I. Doctors who examined the bodies of dead soldiers exposed to mustard gas saw a profound destruction of the soldiers' white blood cells. Although chemical warfare was outlawed after World War I, the United States Department of Defense wondered if these deadly chemicals could be put to some good use. In the 1940s, it commissioned two pharmacists, Louis Goodman and Alfred Gilman, to look into the problem.

Goodman and Gilman reasoned that the profound destruction of a soldier's white blood cells by mustard gas could provide a basis for treatment of white blood cell cancers using weaker versions of mustard gas.

chemotherapeutic drugs, melphalan produces side effects, including hair loss, mouth sores, upset stomach, fatigue, and increased chances of bacterial infections. Most of these side effects reverse once melphalan chemotherapy is stopped.

Once doctors determine that the myeloma cells have been eliminated from the bone marrow of the patient, the frozen healthy bone marrow cells are thawed and re-infused into the patient. This helps restore blood-forming cells to the patient. Patients who receive strong doses of chemotherapy and have their bone marrow replaced can live two to three years longer than patients who only receive chemothcrapy.

Goodman and Gilman first tested their idea on mice. They injected mice with a blood cancer and then injected weaker preparations of mustard gas into the mice to see if this could cure the animal. They were so successful in curing the mice of cancer that they next tried their idea in humans.

Working in collaboration with a surgeon, Gustav Linskog, the two pharmacists gave a patient who had a white blood cell cancer, called non-Hodgkin's lymphoma, a mustard gas derivative named mustine. They immediately saw the patient's tumor shrink. And, although the tumor did come back in a few weeks, this was the first time it was shown that cancers could be effectively treated with chemical poisons. Today newer versions of mustine, along with other powerful cytotoxic drugs, are used to cure cancer or reduce the risk of its recurrence. The recurrence of breast cancer, colon cancer, and lung cancer after surgery has been dramatically lowered using low doses of chemotherapeutic drugs, while childhood **leukemia**, a cancer once considered fatal, is now curable.

TRANSPLANTATION

In some rare cases of myeloma, a patient may have a healthy sibling who is genetically similar and whose bone marrow tissue is a close match. This means that the healthy sibling can give bone marrow tissue to the sick brother or sister. In this situation the physician performs what is called medically an **allogeneic** stem cell transplant. Compared to reinjection of a patient's own frozen bone marrow cells, using bone marrow from a brother or sister offers the advantage that the fresh bone marrow won't contain any possible myeloma cells.

This procedure, however, is not without risk. Up to 20 percent of patients who undergo this treatment have died. Allogeneic transplants require the use of powerful cytotoxic drugs and radiation to completely destroy the myeloma but severely damage healthy bone marrow tissue. During the time that patients undergo chemotherapy and radiation treatment they are extremely vulnerable to all types of common bacterial infections because they have lost all their white blood cells. There is also a risk after infusion of the sibling's white blood cells that they see the patient's normal tissue as foreign and destroy it. This is called graft-versus-host disease. Doctors sometimes try to lessen graft-versus-host disease by attempting "mini" versions of the allogeneic transplant. Mini-allogeneic transplants do not involve destroying all of the patient's bone marrow. Scientists believe this procedure will provide beneficial lymphocytes from the donor, which are able to attack myeloma cells without generating harmful ones that react against normal tissue. The short- and long-term risks with allogeneic transplants are high. Up to half of the patients experience acute or immediate immune reactions after transplant or suffer from long-term slow tissue damage from tissue-reactive donor lymphocytes. Therefore, doctors only consider these risky options appropriate for relatively young patients who have failed to respond to all other treatments.

SUMMARY

For persons diagnosed in an early stage of myeloma who are experiencing pain, anemia-induced fatigue, or an increased number of infections, palliative medical treatment is most often used, including pain-alleviating drugs, bisphosphonates to lessen bone loss, erythropoietin to boost red blood cell production, and antibiotics to prevent bacterial infection. If myeloma progresses to an advanced stage, then chemotherapeutic drugs such as melphalan are employed to reduce or eliminate the number of cancer cells in the patient. Patients are often re-infused with their own blood stem cells after they were cleansed of myeloma cells or in some cases given bone marrow stem cells from a compatible blood donor such as a sibling. While current palliative care, chemotherapy, and bone marrow transplantation will not cure the myeloma, these treatments can offer many patients longer lives with a return to near-normal levels of activity.

7

PROMISING MEDICAL THERAPIES FOR MYELOMA

KEY POINTS

- No cure for myeloma has yet been discovered.

- Doctors are pursuing many promising avenues for new treatments and a cure for myeloma.

- Chemotherapy, immunotherapy, and other substances are among the possibilities under study.

While the use of chemotherapeutic drugs and allogeneic bone marrow transplants discussed in the previous chapter has substantially lessened disease symptoms and lengthened the lives of myeloma patients, there is still no true cure for myeloma. Inevitably, patients see their cancers return, an event called a relapse. Treatment for myeloma relapse is known as salvage therapy. If relapse occurs within six months after stopping chemotherapy, the patient may repeat the chemotherapy to see whether more therapy might be effective. Other options for relapsed disease include participation in clinical trials that involve new experimental drugs. Unlike conventional chemotherapeutic drugs that block DNA replication, many of these new drugs work completely differently. They are based on scientists' new understanding of the biology of myeloma, such as knowledge of the key myeloma growth factors and lymphokines, and insight into myeloma's interaction with bone marrow cells.

The newest and most promising drugs are being tested in the early stages of myeloma when they are theorized to work to give a more powerful effect in combination with older chemotherapy drugs. The clinical benefits of the newer and more widely used experimental drugs are discussed below.

THALIDOMIDE

Thalidomide is a drug that was originally used in the 1950s as a sedative to treat morning sickness in pregnant women. It was quickly removed from pharmacies, however, after it was shown to cause severe birth defects. Recently thalidomide has been found to have a beneficial use as an anti-cancer drug. Thalidomide has the remarkable ability to stop the growth of myeloma tumors that were previously found to be resistant to chemotherapy. After a two-year clinical study, thalidomide treatment showed a 40 percent increase in the number of symptom-free patients compared to patients treated with standard chemotherapy. This was true even in patients with an aggressive and untreatable form of myeloma.

Thalidomide is anti-angiogenic, meaning that it prevents new blood vessels from forming and so starves myeloma cells of both oxygen and vital nutrients. Thalidomide also prevents bone marrow cells from making the myeloma growth factor IL-6. Thalidomide alters how myeloma cells interact with bone marrow cells, essentially by lessening

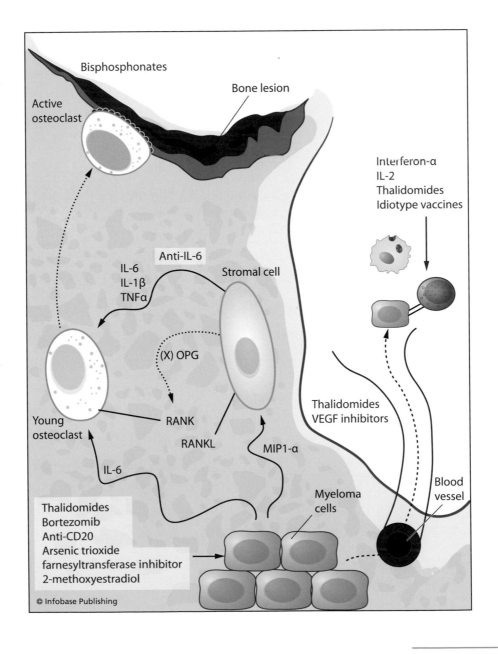

◆ DOES A POUND OF SHARK CARTILAGE A DAY KEEP THE CANCER AWAY?

In 1983 two doctors, Anne Lee and Robert Langer, reported that proteins found in shark cartilage stopped the growth of new blood vessels around cancer cells. Since then numerous other scientific papers have reported similar properties of proteins found in shark cartilage. Shark cartilage was later found to contain a protein called angiogenin, which can stop new blood vessels from forming and starve a tumor of oxygen and blood nutrients. In theory, angiogenin seemed to be a helpful treatment for many cancers, including myeloma. Today dozens of products containing shark cartilage are sold in the marketplace as a "natural cancer cure" with sales in the millions of dollars, but are they really effective? Doctors have tested this idea in clinics with cancer patients. Unfortunately, there is no conclusive evidence that shark cartilage, when eaten as a food supplement, can stop cancer in humans. The reason for failure is that angiogenin is a large, complex protein that will not easily pass into the blood from the intestine unless it is first broken down into small pieces by digestive enzymes, at which point it loses all function. Thus, shark cartilage supplements are useless when eaten.

contact between these two cell types and thus by preventing bone marrow cells from providing survival signals to myeloma cells. As a result of thalidomide's actions, myeloma cells become more prone to

Figure 7.1   *(opposite page)* Here you can see how a few of the latest drugs are used to fight myeloma.

undergo apoptosis. Thalidomide can also boost beneficial lymphokines and decrease harmful ones. Thalidomide induces bone cells to make interferon and interleukin-2. These lymphokines can activate cytotoxic T cells and NK cells and cause them to kill myeloma cells better. Thalidomide also stops overproduction of TNF-α. If TNF-α is produced in high amounts, it weakens bone marrow and causes neutrophils and lymphocytes to die, or inhibits the production of red blood cells. Lowering TNF-α levels can therefore help the immune system and bone marrow return to normal and fight infection or reverse anemia.

Because thalidomide shows few side effects, other than the occasional blood clot or dizziness and numbness in the arms and legs, it has gained greater use in the clinic for myeloma treatment.

BORTEZOMIB

Bortezomib, or more commonly known as Velcade, is a drug that also stops myeloma cells from growing but, unlike melphalan and many other chemotherapeutic drugs, it does not damage the cell's DNA. It does not block myeloma growth but works by blocking the destruction of old proteins, causing the cell to undergo cell death by apoptosis. Old proteins are normally shredded into small pieces within the cell in barrel-like structures called **proteasomes**. A protein enters one end of the proteasome and is sliced into smaller units to be disposed of or recycled into new protein building blocks. The proteasome keeps the cell in metabolic balance and is important in controlling cell growth. Stopping the proteasome causes a metabolic imbalance in the cell and triggers apoptosis.

Besides inducing apoptosis, bortezomib is also thought to lower the ability of myeloma cells to stick to other bone marrow cells. It makes myeloma cells more sensitive to conventional chemotherapy drugs that also induce apoptosis.

Bortezomib has recently been approved by the U.S. Food and Drug Administration for use in treating multiple myeloma when all other treatments have failed. However, further work and monitoring of patients must be done to determine whether it is safe and effective in the long term in myeloma patients. In patients who have experienced a relapse of myeloma, doctors have found in experimental trials that bortezomib reduced the number of myeloma cells in 35 percent of these patients and allowed them to live nearly 16 months longer compared to patients who did not take bortezomib. Remarkably, 10 percent of the patients who took bortezomib had a complete or nearly complete arrest of their myeloma, which gives added hope to doctors and patients that bortezomib will constitute an important treatment or perhaps even a cure for myeloma.

IMMUNOTHERAPY

Immunotherapy uses the body's immune system to fight cancer. It has the advantage over many chemotherapeutic drugs by having fewer side effects. Immunotherapy relies upon the immune system's ability to identify cancer molecules made only in myeloma cells and to design immune molecules. It is also possible to grow immune cells in the lab that target myeloma-specific cancer molecules and kill myeloma cells. Nowhere is the effectiveness of immunotherapy more apparent than in the use of monoclonal antibodies to treat cancer.

In theory, the creation of a clinically useful antibody is quite simple. First, a B cell that makes the desired antibody is isolated. Then a scientist generates identical B cell **clones** that make large amounts of the antibody in question. These antibodies can be used to recognize

◆ MONOCLONAL ANTIBODIES,
HEY, WHO NEEDS THEM?

Like many great discoveries, the discovery of the monoclonal antibody came by chance. César Milstein was born in 1927 in Argentina. After earning a Ph.D. in biochemistry from the University of Buenos Aires, he won a scholarship to study the structure of antibody molecules at the University of Cambridge in Britain. At that time, little was known about antibody structure. As hard as scientists tried, no one could get a clear picture of the shape of an antibody molecule. Dr. Milstein was convinced that the antibody structure could be resolved if he looked at how a B cell made antibodies. To do this he needed to grow a single B cell into many identical cell clones in a test tube. This was not an easy task, because B cells do not grow or divide well in the test tube and soon die. As luck would have it, he met and became good friends with Dr. Georges Köhler, who had just arrived at the University of Cambridge from Switzerland. The two became friends, and Köhler told Milstein about a technique he learned in Switzerland that could isolate a single B cell as it made its individual antibody from a blood sample containing thousands of B cells. Together Köhler and Milstein devised a way to fuse a cancer cell, which can be easily grown and divides for years in a test tube, with a normal antibody-producing B cell. The scientists gave this newly formed cell the properties of both continuous cell division in culture and the ability to make large amounts of the original antibody. Using Köhler's technique to isolate a particular B cell and their technique to fuse cells together, Köhler and Milstein could now make many identical clones from a single B cell that grew continuously and made one, unique antibody.

At the time, their technique seemed so simple that few fellow scientists grasped its importance. In fact, one government scientist said after reviewing their work, "It is certainly difficult for us to identify any immediate practical applications which could be pursued as a commercial venture, even assuming that publication [of their technique] had not already occurred." Today Drs. Milstein and Köhler's technique of making a single kind of antibody from B cell clones, called the monoclonal antibody technique, has become an essential method to cre-

Figure 7.2 César Milstein was one of the developers of the monoclonal antibody technique, for which he and Dr. Georges Köhler were awarded the Nobel Prize in Medicine and Physiology in 1984. (© Dr. Rob Stepney/Photo Researchers, Inc.)

ate many antibodies for medical testing and to treat cancers, including myeloma. This invention was so revolutionary that in 1984 Drs. Milstein and Köhler were awarded the Nobel Prize in Medicine and Physiology for their work.

and destroy only cancer cells and leave healthy, normal tissue intact. Such antibodies can be used by themselves to kill cells or attached to chemotherapy drugs to deliver their deadly drug payload to the tumor.

Myeloma patients in some experimental drug trials are given injections of antibodies that recognize interleukin-6 and deprive myeloma cells of the growth-stimulating effects of interleukin-6. Other experimental trials involve injecting patients with an antibody against a common B cell molecule called CD20. When an antibody binds to a CD20 that is found on the cell surface of B cells, it signals to the cell to die by apoptosis. Both kinds of antibodies have shown some beneficial effects in myeloma patients.

Most people mistakenly think that the sole purpose of the immune system is to ward off viral and bacterial infections, but in reality its role is far more extensive. NK cells of the innate immune system are very effective at recognizing and eliminating cancer cells from the body before they become a problem. Occasionally, however, cancer cells spread too rapidly and overwhelm the immune system. In other cases, cancer cells acquire the ability to hide themselves from the immune system. Medical researchers who study the NK cells, the immune system, and myeloma are devoting their best efforts to develop a therapy based on lymphokines to treat myeloma. The two lymphokines thought to be most beneficial for the treatment of myeloma are interferon-α and interleukin-2. Interferon-α has been shown to be effective in keeping myeloma progression stable in patients after their chemotherapy. Patients who are treated with interferon-α live longer and are free of many myeloma-related symptoms compared with ones who did not receive interferon-α. Numerous medical studies have demonstrated the great potential of interleukin-2 to treat cancer. Interleukin-2 boosts the growth of both cytotoxic T cells and NK cells that are then better able seek out and kill cancer cells. Interleukin-2 has been shown to reduce the number of myeloma cells in patients.

Another experimental approach is to use a vaccine made from M protein. Because M protein is the antibody that is made only in the myeloma cell, it can be used to generate cytotoxic T cells in the patient's blood that recognize and eliminate their myeloma cells. Early results from experimental trials have shown that M protein vaccination might be a viable way to make designer T cells that stop the growth of a patient's myeloma. One potential problem with the **vaccine** approach is that the same M protein used to vaccinate a patient is already found in large amounts in the blood of myeloma patients. These high levels of M protein might interfere with attempts to generate new cytotoxic T cells that react to the M protein and myeloma cells. More work will be needed to elucidate the benefits of such M protein vaccination and show whether this approach is better than other treatments.

ANGIOGENIC INHIBITORS

The growth of new blood vessels, or **angiogenesis**, is an important means by which cancers grow and spread. Cancer cells must have oxygen and nutrients supplied by blood and blood vessels to grow. Blood vessels also let cancer cells travel and spread to distant sites in the body. A protein called vascular endothelial growth factor (VEGF) is made by myeloma cells and plays a key role in the spread of myeloma. VEGF stimulates new blood vessel formation and increases myeloma cell movement into neighboring blood vessels and tissues. Blocking VEGF actions would stop blood vessel formation and inhibit myeloma spread. Therefore, scientists have begun clinical trials to test whether drugs that block VEGF can prevent new blood vessel formation and stop myeloma disease.

SUMMARY

These are exciting times in the care and treatment of patients with myeloma. Breakthrough drug treatments, like thalidomide and bortezomib, eliminate myeloma in ways different from conventional chemotherapy and are based on a new understanding of the biology of myeloma. Medical scientists are also attacking myeloma using drugs that starve the cancer of oxygen and nutrients, designing customized antibodies to deliver death-inducing drugs or using lymphokines to boost the ability of NK and cytotoxic T cells to seek out and destroy myeloma cell. It is hoped that these new approaches for the treatment of myeloma can allow doctors and patients to hope that, if not cured, myeloma patients can live longer and normal lives.

Despite recent advancements in cancer therapy and new insights into the biology of multiple myeloma, the chances of a true cure are still low. This does not mean there is no hope. Ongoing clinical trials promise to improve palliative care, expand further the roles of current drugs, and better transplantation outcomes such that individuals afflicted with myeloma can live longer and near-normal lives for years if diagnosed and treated early.

So where do we go from here?

Physicians and other medical scientists are now following two paths of exploration. One path is to improve myeloma response in patients using a more intense use of current treatments. The other path is to convert this deadly disease into one that is managed for the long term, much like diabetes. Success on either path will require a better understanding of myeloma biology and its complex interaction with bone and blood cells. We must screen for this disease earlier, before symptoms arise, myeloma growth is irreversible, and damage has already been done, so that patient has a better chance of fighting the disease.

So in the future when the doctor says the dreaded words *multiple myeloma cancer*, patients will have treatment options and possible cures for this now deadly disease. Success on either path will be momentous!

GLOSSARY

♦

adaptive immune system   The arm of the immune system that is comprised of T and B cells, which can generate a new and novel protective mechanism in individuals newly exposed to a particular pathogen or foreign substance.

albumin   A major blood protein synthesized by the liver and responsible for blood viscosity and the transport of body fats and hormones.

allogencic   Cells that are from the same species but are genetically different. For example, blue and brown eye colors are each produced by a common set of genes that contain only small changes or differences.

amino acids   Cellular molecules that form the basic building blocks of proteins.

anemia   A reduction in the number of red blood cells causing symptoms of weakness and fatigue.

angiogenesis   The formation of blood vessels

antibodies   Y-shaped protein molecules produced by B cells, constituting a primary immune defense weapon of the immune system. Each antibody molecule has a unique binding site that can combine with its complementary site, which is found on a foreign substance or microbe.

antigen   A foreign substance comprised usually of protein or sugar chains that stimulate the immune system to produce complementary antibodies.

apoptosis   A cellular process by which a cell commits suicide; and the cellular process is marked by the cutting up of the cell's genetic material into small pieces.

B cell (or B-lymphocyte)   A cell found in the immune system that has the function of making antibodies.

bacteria   Microscopic single-celled spherical, spiral, or rod-shaped organisms that are involved in fermentation, spoilage of food, or infectious diseases.

Bence Jones protein   A protein composed of one or two antibody light chains, found in high concentration in the urine of patients with multiple myeloma.

benign   The property of having little or no harmful effects. For example, warts are a harmless, or benign, form of tumor.

bisphosphonate   A class of drugs used to inhibit bone loss in cancer patients.

bone marrow   The soft, red- or yellow-colored tissue that fills most bone cavities and is the source of red blood cells and white blood cells.

bortezomib   A class of drugs used to inhibit cancer cell growth by causing the cell to undergo suicide.

buffy coat   The white layer of white blood cells that forms when blood clots or blood is spun at high speed in a centrifuge.

cancer   A malignant and invasive growth of cells.

cells   The smallest structural and functional units of a plant or animal. Cells consist of a nucleus containing genetic material, surrounded by cytoplasm where proteins are synthesized, and an outer semipermeable membrane.

chemotherapy   A form of medical treatment in which drugs are administered to kill cancer cells.

chromosomes   Thread-like structures that encode the cell's genetic material. Humans have 23 pairs of chromosomes designated 1 to 22, plus one pair of sex chromosomes called X and Y, which determines whether a person is male or female.

chromosome diploid   The cell's state of having a normal set (or number) of chromosomes, with one half of the chromosomes coming from the mother and the other half from the father. The diploid number in human cells is 46, or 23 chromosomes from each parent.

chromosome trisomy   The condition of having three copies of a given chromosome in a cell rather than the normal number of two chromosomes.

clones   A group of genetically identical cells.

complement   A group of proteins found in the blood that reacts to antibodies bound to bacteria, having the ability to make holes in the bacterial cell wall.

computerized axial tomography (CAT) scan   A method of examining body organs by first scanning them with X rays and using a computer to reconstruct a three-dimensional image of the organs.

C-reactive protein   A protein produced by the liver that increases in concentration in the blood during infection and cancer.

creatinine   A cellular waste product formed during energy production in the cell. High amounts of creatinine are produced in muscle tissue and removed from the body in the urine.

cytoplasm   Cellular protoplasm found between the outer cell membrane and the cell nucleus. Cytoplasm contains enzymes, structural proteins and salts to support cell shape and cell metabolism.

cytotoxic T cell   A member of the T cell family that eliminates cancer cells or cells infected with virus.

dendritic cell   A cell found in the lymph nodes, blood, or spleen that traps foreign particles or proteins and presents them to T cells.

deoxyribonucleic acid (DNA)   A helical double-stranded molecule that encodes all inherited characteristics or genes.

electrophoresis   A laboratory procedure using an electric field to separate molecules based on their differences in mass (or weight).

epidemiologists   Scientists who work in the branch of medicine that studies the occurrence and causes of various diseases in the human population.

epitope   The portion of a foreign substance that is recognized by an antibody.

erythrocytes   Commonly called red blood cells, these contain hemoglobin to carry oxygen throughout the body.

erythropoietin   A protein hormone that stimulates bone marrow to produce red blood cells.

extramedullary   Located or taking place outside the bone marrow.

genes   The basic units of inheritance, which provide the cell with instructions to produce proteins.

helper T cell   A T cell group member that signals and aids B cells to produce antibodies.

hemodialysis   A medical procedure used to remove metabolic waste products from the body using a dialysis machine.

hemoglobin   A red protein found in red blood cells that transports oxygen from the lungs to distant body tissues.

human leukocyte antigen (HLA)   A complex set of inherited genes that encode cell surface proteins and allows the immune systems to distinguish the body's own cells from another person's cells.

hormone   A small molecule comprised of a short chain of amino acids or a steroid that conveys growth or metabolic signals.

hypercalcemia   The disease state of having an abnormally large amount of calcium in the blood.

immune system   A complex network of interacting cells, lymphokines and blood-forming tissues that protect the body from disease pathogens, foreign substances and cancer cells.

innate immune system   The "inborn" arm of the immune system that is comprised of macrophage, neutrophils, and complement, and protects us from bacterial infection.

interferon-α   A protein produced by cells of the immune system in response to viral infection to block replication of the virus.

interleukin-2 (IL-2)   A member of the lymphokine protein family produced by cells of the immune systems that regulate T- and B-cell growth.

interleukin-6 (IL-6)   A member of the lymphokine protein family produced by cells of the immune systems that regulate cell growth, metabolism, and myeloma growth factor.

light chain (antibody light chain)   One of a pair of short polypeptide chains that comprise the two arms of the antibody molecule. These are classified as one of two types: lambda or kappa.

leukemia A type of blood cancer characterized by the unrestrained proliferation of white blood cells.

leukocyte Also known as a white blood cell. Leukocytes circulate in the blood and spleen to cleanse the blood and protect it from infection.

lymph nodes Small round organs that contain large numbers of lymphocytes. Lymph nodes are the major site where lymphocytes see, react, and remove bacteria and foreign particles from the body.

lymphocyte A set of small colorless cells comprised of B and T cells, forming the adaptive arm of the immune system.

lymphokines Proteins expressed and secreted by cells of the immune system that act to regulate the immune system.

macrophages Large amoeba-like white blood cells that ingest foreign particles and bacteria by the process of phagocytosis.

magnetic resonance imaging (MRI) A noninvasive diagnostic procedure that can produce computerized images of internal body tissues. MRI is based on the changes in an atom's spin because of the application of strong radio waves.

malignant A form of cancer characterized by the uncontrolled growth and spread of cancer cells throughout the body.

melphalan An anti-cancer drug used to treat multiple myeloma.

microbe A microscopic organism generally thought of as a bacterium that causes disease.

β_2-microglobulin A small protein normally found on the surface of healthy cells but is released into the blood by cancer cells.

molecules The smallest units of a substance, composed of two or more atoms that are held together by chemical forces.

morphine A powerful derivative of opium that is used to relieve pain or induce sleep.

M protein An abnormal form of antibody that is produced by myeloma cells and found in high amounts in the blood of persons diagnosed with myeloma.

myeloma A malignant form of cancer localized in the bone marrow and comprised of mature B cells called plasma cells.

natural killer (NK) cells Cells of the immune system that can destroy virus-infected or cancerous cells without any prior exposure or signals from other immune system cells.

neoplasm An abnormal new growth of tissue also referred to as a tumor.

neutrophils White blood cells characterized by grainy-looking cytoplasm. They protect the body by ingesting bacteria.

non-Hodgkin's lymphoma A form of white blood cell cancer derived from the B-lymphocyte population.

opioids A group of natural substances used to relieve pain.

opium A highly addictive drug derived from the opium poppy, which produces a feeling of well-being, hallucinations, and drowsiness.

organs A defined group of tissues that form large structures in our body and include the liver, heart, and kidney.

osteoblasts Bone-forming cells.

osteoclasts Cells found in the bone marrow that remove old and weakened bone tissue.

palliative care A form of medical treatment that relieves only the symptoms of a disease without producing a cure.

phagocytosis   The amoeboid-like process of engulfing and ingesting bacteria or foreign particles by macrophage cells.

plasma   The liquid portion of the blood, devoid of blood cells, and which contains clotting factors, salts, and body nutrients.

plasma cells   Mature B cells that make and secrete large amounts of antibody molecules.

plasmablasts   The precursor B cell type that change into mature plasma cells.

platelets   Microscopic disc-shaped particles found in the blood plasma that promote the formation of blood clots.

pluripotents   A primordial cell type found in the bone marrow that can change into more specialized cell types.

pre-B cell   An early stage of B-cell development when the B cell does not yet secrete antibody.

pro-B cell   The earliest stage in a B cell's development wherein the B cell still cannot synthesize antibody molecules.

proteasomes   Barrel-shaped complexes of proteins found inside the cell cytoplasm that serve to digest old or worn-out cell proteins.

protons   The positively charged elements of the nucleus of an atom.

reticular cells   Cells that form the scaffolding structure found in bone marrow, blood vessels, or lymph nodes.

somatic hypermutation   A change that occurs in mature B cells in the genes that encode the amino acids of the antigen-antibody binding site, leading to stronger antigen binding by the antibody molecule.

stem cell   A primordial cell that can give rise to all the cells of the immune system, including red and white blood cells.

stromal cells   Cells found in the bone marrow that support the growth and maturation of B cells.

subendosteum   The region of bone marrow adjacent to the inner bone surface.

T cell   A principal type of white blood cell, also called a T lymphocyte. T cells mature in the thymus gland and destroy virus-infected cells. They also help B cells to grow and produce antibody molecules.

T cell receptors   Principal molecules found on the surface of T cells that allow the T cell to recognize pathogens.

thalidomide   A drug that was formerly used as a sedative for pregnant women but caused severe abnormalities in the fetus. Thalidomide is used in myeloma patients to control cancer growth or the formation of blood vessels found in myeloma tumors.

thymus   A butterfly-shaped gland found at the base of the neck that is the site of T cell growth and development.

tissues   A grouping of similar cell types that form well-defined structures and perform common functions, for example, muscle, lung, or nerve tissue.

tumors   Uncontrolled and abnormal growths of cells.

vaccine   A substance isolated from bacteria or viruses that is injected into the body to induce protection, or inoculate, against that particular bacterial or viral disease.

vascular endothelial growth factor (VEGF)   Growth factor produced by stromal cells and tumor cells that promote the formation of new blood vessels.

VDJ recombinase complex   Enzyme found in B cells that joins segments of the immunoglobulin genes together so that the B cell can
produce antibody protein.

vertebroplasty   A medical procedure that involves the fusion of bone
using material similar to that of white dental filling.

virus   A submicroscopic particle that often causes disease. Viruses
consist of genetic material surrounded by a protein coat. Viruses are
unable to reproduce without the help of a host cell and are therefore
considered to be nonliving.

white blood cell   A white or clear cell found in the blood that helps
protect the body from infections and disease. White blood cells are
also called leukocytes.

FURTHER RESOURCES

◆

Books and Articles

Chapter 1

Janeway, Jr., C.A., P. Travers, M. Walport, and M.J. Schlomchik. *Immunobiology: The immune system in health and disease.* New York: Garland Science Publishing, 2005.

Learoyd, P. "A short history of blood transfusion," *National Blood Service Leeds Blood Center* (January 2006): 1–18.

Paul, W.E. *Fundamental Immunology.* Hagerstown, Md.: Lippicott Williams and Wilkins, 2003.

Chapter 2

Milstein, C. "With the benefit of hindsight." *Immunology Today* 21, 8 (August 2000): 359–364.

McHeyzer-Williams, L.J., and M.G. McHeyzer-Williams. "Antigen-specific memory B cell development." *Annual Review of Immunology* 2, 8 (August 2005): 487–513.

O'Connor, B.P., M.W. Gleeson, R.J. Noelle, and L.D. Erickson. "The rise and fall of long-lived humoral immunity: Terminal differentiation of plasma cells in health and disease," *Immunology Reviews* 194 (August 2003): 61–76.

Chapter 3

Benjamin, M., S. Reddy, and O.W. Brawley. "Myeloma and race: a review of the literature," *Cancer Metastasis Reviews* 22, 1 (March 2003): 87–93.

Blattner, W.A., Blair, A., and Mason, T.J. "Multiple myeloma in the United States, 1950 to 1975," *Cancer* 48, no 11 (December 1981): 2547–2554.

Neriishi, K., Nakashima, E., and Suzuki G. "Monoclonal gammopathy of undetermined significance in atomic bomb survivors: Incidence and transformation to multiple myeloma," *British Journal of Haematology* 121, 3 (2003): 405–410.

Steven, F.J., A. Solomon, and M. Schiffer. "Bence Jones Proteins: Powerful Tool for Fundamental Study of Protein Chemistry and Pathophysiology." Available online. URL: http://:www.osti.gov/bridge/servlets/purl/10185739-MwMbkx/10185739.PDF. Downloaded on October 20, 2006.

Chapter 4

Hideshima, T., P.L. Bergsagel, W.M. Kuehl, and K.C. Anderson. "Advances in biology of multiple myeloma: Clinical applications," *Blood* 104, 3 (January 2004): 607–618.

Lauta, V.M. "A review of the cytokine network in multiple myeloma: diagnostic, prognostic, and therapeutic implications," *Cancer* 97, 10 (August 2003): 2440–2452.

Ludwig, H. "Advances in biology and treatment of multiple myeloma," *Annals of Oncology* 16, 2 (2005): Supplement: 106–112.

Magrangeas, F., L. Lode, S. Wuilleme, S. Minvielle, and H. Avet-Loiseau. "Genetic heterogeneity in multiple myeloma," *Leukemia* 19, 2 (February 2005): 191–194.

Roodman, G.D. "Pathogenesis of myeloma bone disease," *Blood Cells, Molecules and Diseases* 32, 2 (March 2003): 290–292.

Seidl, S., H. Kaufmann, and J. Drach. "New insights into the pathophysiology of multiple myeloma," *Lancet Oncology* 4, 9 (September 2003): 557–564.

Sirohi, B., and R. Powles. "Multiple myeloma," *Lancet* 363, 9412 (March 2004): 875–887.

Chapter 5

Angtuaco, E.J., A.B. Fassas, R. Walker, R. Sethi, and B. Barlogie. "Multiple myeloma: Clinical review and diagnostic imaging 2," *Radiology* 231, 1 (April 2004): 11–23.

Calarco, J. "An Historical Overview of the Discovery of the X-Ray," Yale-New Haven Teachers Institute. Available online. URL: http://www.yale.edu/ynhti/. Downloaded on October 20, 2006.

Freitas, R.A., Jr. *Nanomedicine, Volume I: Basic Capabilities*. Austin, Tex.: Landes Bioscience Publishing, 1999.

Gould, T.A. "How MRI Works." Available online. URL: http://health.howstuff-works.com/mri1.htm. Downloaded on November 21, 2006.

Harris. T. "How CAT-scans Work." Available online. URL: http://health.howstuff-works.com/cat-scan.htm. Downloaded on November 21, 2006.

Kyle, R.A., and S.V. Rajkumar. "Monoclonal gammopathies of undetermined significance." *Hematolology/Oncology Clinics North America* 13, 6 (December 1999): 1181–1202.

Mahoney, M.C., Lawvere, S., Falkner, K.L., Averkin Y.I., Ostapenko, V.A., Michalek, A. M., Moysich, K.B. and P.L. McCarthy. "Thyroid cancer incidence trends in Belarus: Examining the impact of Chernobyl," *Cancer* 33, 5 (October 2004): 1025–1033.

Wei, A., and S. Juneja. "Bone marrow immunohistology of plasma cell neoplasms," *Journal of Clinical Pathology* 56, 6 (June 2003): 406–411.

Chapter 6

Barille-Nion, S., B. Barlogie, R. Bataille, P.L. Bergsagel, J. Epstein, R.G. Fenton, J. Jacobson, W.M. Kuehl, J. Shaughnessy, and G. Tricot. "Advances in biology and therapy of multiple myeloma," *Hematology* (American Society Hematology Education Program) (2003): 248–278.

Gibson, J., P.J. Ho, and D. Joshua. "Evolving transplant options for multiple myeloma: Autologous and nonmyeloablative allogenic." *Transplant Proceedings* 36, 8 (October 2004): 2501–2503.

Goodman, L.S., Wintrobe, M.M., Dameshek, W., Goodman, M.J., Gilman, A. and M.T. McLennan. "Landmark article September 21, 1946, Nitrogen mustard therapy. Use of methyl-bis(beta-chloroethyl)amine hydrochloride and tris(beta-chloroethyl)amine hydrochloride for Hodgkin's disease, lymphosarcoma, leukemia, and certain allied and miscellaneous disorders," *Journal of the American Medical Association* 251, 17 (May 1984): 2255–2261.

Harousseau, J.L. "High-dose therapy in multiple myeloma," *Annals of Oncology* 13, 3 (2002) Supplement 4:49–54.

Heffner, L.T., Jr., and S. Lonial "Breakthroughs in the management of multiple myeloma," *Drugs* 63, 16 (2003):1621–1636.

Kyle, R.A., and S.V. Rajkumar. "Multiple myeloma," *New England Journal of Medicine* 351, 18 (October 2004): 1860–1873.

Kumar, A. "Management of multiple myeloma: A systematic review and critical appraisal of published studies," *Lancet Oncology* 4, 5 (May 2005):293–304.

Morgan, G. J., and F. E. Davies. "Evolving treatment strategies for myeloma," *British Journal of Cancer* 92, 2 (January 2005): 217–221.

Tricot, G., B. Barlogie, and F. van Rhee. "Treatment advances in multiple myeloma," *British Journal of Haematology* 125, 1 (January 2004): 24–30.

Chapter 7

Boccadoro, M., and A. Palumbo. "New developments and treatment in multiple myeloma: New drugs in the treatment of multiple myeloma," *Annals of Oncology* 13 (2002): Supplement 4:55–58.

Boye, J., T. Elter, and A. Engert. "An overview of the current clinical use of the anti-CD20 monoclonal antibody rituximab," *Annals of Oncology* 14, 4 (April 2003): 520–535.

Bruno, B., M. Rotta, L. Giaccone, M. Massaia, A. Bertola, A. Palumbo, and M. Boccadoro. "New drugs for treatment of multiple myeloma," *Lancet Oncology* 5, 7 (July 2004): 430–442.

Chauhan, D., T. Hideshima, C. Mitsiades, P. Richardson, and K.C. Anderson. "Proteasome inhibitor therapy in multiple myeloma," *Molecular Cancer Therapy* 4, 4 (April 2005): 686–692.

Drach, J., and H. Kaufmann. "New developments and treatment in multiple myeloma: new insights on molecular biology," *Annals of Oncology* 13 (2002): Supplement 4: 43–47.

Harrison, S.J., and G. Cook. " Immunotherapy in multiple myeloma—possibility or probability?" *British Journal of Haematology* 130, 3 (August 2005): 344–362.

Hideshima, T., P. Richardson, and K.C. Anderson. "Novel therapeutic approaches for multiple myeloma," *Immunology Reviews* 194 (August 2003):164–176.

Lee, A., and R. Langer. "Shark cartilage contains inhibitors of tumor angiogenesis," *Science* 221, 1416 (September 1983): 1185–1187.

Pagnucco, G., G. Cardinale, and F. Gervasi. "Targeting multiple myeloma cells and their bone marrow microenvironment," *Annals of the New York Academy of Science* 1028 (December 2004): 390–399.

Stanford, B.L., and S.D. Zondor. "Bortezomib treatment for multiple myeloma," *Annals of Pharmacotherapy* 37, 12 (December 2003): 1825–1830.

Strasser, K., and H. Ludwig. "Thalidomide treatment in multiple myeloma," *Blood Reviews* 16, 4 (December 2002): 207–215.

Trikha, M., R. Corringham, B. Klein, and J.F. Rossi. "Targeted anti-interleukin-6 monoclonal antibody therapy for cancer: A review of the rationale and clinical evidence," *Clinical Cancer Reseach* 9, 13 (October 2003): 4653–4665.

Voorhees, P.M., E.C. Dees, B. O'Neil, and R.Z. Orlowski. "The proteasome as a target for cancer therapy," *Clinical Cancer Research* 9, 17 (December 2003): 6316–6325.

Web Sites

Following are resources and publications to provide additional information for those interested in increasing their understanding of myeloma.

General Medicine

Mayo Clinic

http://www.mayoclinic.com

MedicineNet.com
http://www:medicinenet.com

Medscape
http://www.medscape.com

National Institutes of Health
http://www.nih.gov

National Library of Medicine
http://www.ncbi.nlm.nih.gov

WebMD
http://www.webmd.com

Cancer Organizations

American Cancer Society
http://www.cancer.org

Cancer Information Network
http://www.cancerlinksusa.com

Mayo Clinic
http://www.mayoclinic.org

National Cancer Institute
http://www.cancer.gov

The Leukemia & Lymphoma Society
http://www.lls.org

Myeloma Organizations

International Myeloma Foundation
http://www.myeloma.org/

The Multiple Myeloma Research Foundation
http://www.multiplemyeloma.org/

Myeloma Clinical Trials

National Institutes of Heath
http://www.clinicaltrials.gov

National Cancer Institute
http://www.cancer.gov/clinical_trials/

INDEX

♦

ABOUT THE AUTHOR

◆

JEROME E. TANNER is the cofounder and scientific director at the biotechnology company TanTec Biosystems, located in Montreal, Quebec. Born in Cincinnati, Ohio, he earned his bachelor's degree in biology from the University of Cincinnati and his Ph.D. from the University of Chicago, specializing in immunology and cancer-causing viruses. Dr. Tanner has studied how immune cells communicate and fight virus infection and certain blood cancers, both at the U.S. Food and Drug Administration and National Institutes of Health, and later as an assistant professor at the University of Ottawa in Ontario, Canada. Dr. Tanner has coauthored more than 30 scientific publications and monographs in the areas of virus research and immunology and was awarded two patents for his work on cancer vaccines and cancer detection.

In Dr. Tanner's current position as president and scientific director at TanTec Biosystems Inc., he continues to make important advances in the field of cancer treatment by combining his interests in cancer, viruses, and the application of antibody therapy toward the treatment of cancer and life-threatening infectious diseases.